NORTHWEST PASSAGE SOLO

Northwest Passage Solo

BY DAVID SCOTT COWPER

with David Pelly

Seafarer Books

Sheridan House

First published in the United States of America 1994
by Sheridan House Inc.
145 Palisade Street
Dobbs Ferry, NY 10522

Published in the United Kingdom by Seafarer Books

Library of Congress Cataloging-in-Publication Data

Cowper, David Scott,
    Northwest passage solo / David Scott Cowper.
        p.   cm.
    ISBN 0-924488-65-1 : $23.95
    1. Cowper, David Scott—Journeys.   2. Mabel E. Holland (Boat)
3. Northwest Passage.   4. Canada, Northern—Description and travel.
5. Sailing, Single-handed.   I. Title.
0670 1986.C69   1994
910'.9063' 27—dc20   93-3441
                                                                 CIP

Printed in Great Britain

ISBN 0-924486-65-1

Cover Design by Louis MacKay
Maps by Walter Kemsley
Diagram by Trevor Ridley
Photographs by the Author

Contents

Acknowledgements

I am deeply indebted to the following for their support and contributions, all of which helped to make my transit of the Northwest Passage a success. Although this voyage was done singlehanded, it still required the help and support of many people. I have never failed to be surprised when help from the most unexpected quarters has come totally out of the blue. When compiling such lists there is always another name that should have been included and to anyone I may have overlooked I extend humble apologies and assure them that it has been unintentional.

I would like to pay a special tribute to Beryl Turner my secretary *cum* voyage co-ordinator who has worked tirelessly on my behalf writing letters, reports and news bulletins, packing up many items for the boat, compiling countless lists of equipment, indexing and cross-referencing charts and who was on call 24 hours per day to receive my calls for assistance from distant parts of the world.

I would also like to thank David Pelly for working so patiently and tirelessly to assemble this book from all the notes and scribbles that I presented to him and making sense of it all.

My thanks are particularly due to the following individuals and institutions:-

The late Captain Tom Pullen, Barry Vickers, Captain Alan Smith, The Port of Tyne, Neville Trotter MP, The Royal National Lifeboat Institution, Frederika Semotiuk, Bob

Browne, The Canadian Goverment and Canadian Coastguard, Bezal and Terry Jesudason, Buster Welsh, Larry Solar, Admiral Ilg USN, Christian Wan of Taylor Smith Shipyard, Bruce Perkins of Perkins Shipping, Norman and Kay Turner, Captain James Mayor, Pat Gaulton, John Goodman, Sir Charles Blois, Capt Claude Guimont, the Rev David Holloway, who blessed the boats before each circumnavigation.

Barratts, Bridon Ropes, Callers Pegasus, Cleghorn Waring, Chloride Automotive Batteries, Deep Sea Seals, Everbright Fastners, FKI Communications, Glasby Pharmaceuticals, Paul Gardner Engineering, Henshaw Inflatables Ltd., International Paints, John Lilley and Gillie, John Nixon Plant Sales, Kelvin Hughes, Lucas CAV, *Maersk Ascension*, Munster Sims, Neco Marine, North British Tapes, Northern Transportation Co.Ltd., Nott & James, Optimus, Plessey, Pump International, Thomas Reed & Sons, Rockford Marine Enterprises, S.A.Equipment, Scottish and Newcastle Breweries, Service Welding, Simpson Lawrence, Swire Pacific, Tirfor, Tynecolor Ltd., James Walker and Sons, Wallas Stoves, C.Westin, Benjamin R.Vickers & Sons.

Barbour, Boots, Murdoch Morrison of Blacks Camping and Leisure, Phoenix, Tony Morgan MK Ltd., Ultimate, Baxters, Brook Bond Foods, Beecham Foods, Colmans Foods, J.A.Sharwood, William Grant & Sons.

And all the radio hams who 'worked me' across the ocean.

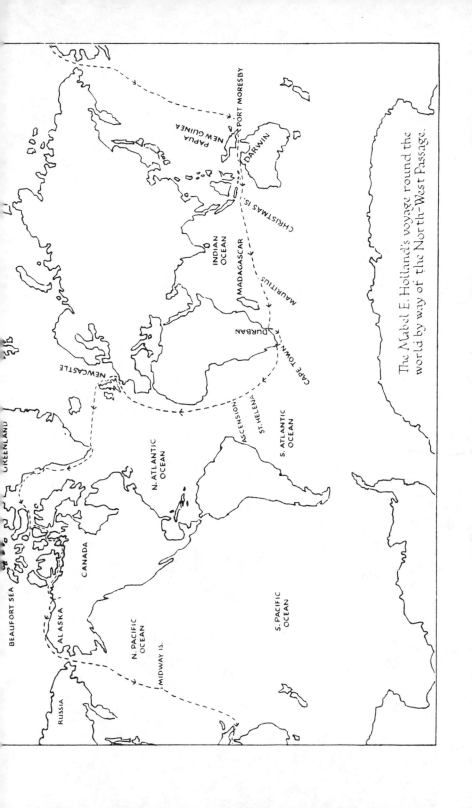

The Mabel E. Holland's voyage round the world by way of the North-West Passage.

Chapter 1

The tantalizing goal

IN thick fog and fading light, the ice took me by surprise. A series of jarring impacts brought my converted lifeboat *Mabel E.Holland* to a standstill as she ran into pack-ice of nine-tenths density: a heaving, swaying wilderness of broken slabs whose jagged edges ground against each other and the sides of the boat with a frighteningly ugly sound. I put both engines full astern in an effort to back out into open water but it was too late. The strong wind had quickly brought more ice in astern and I was now completely beset. Being so close to the magnetic North Pole, the compass had lost all direction and swung in aimless circles. Like the compass needle, I was completely disoriented. There was nothing more to be done except shut down the engines and let the ice take the initiative.

It was impossible to rest as the cabin thermometer sank below zero and the wooden hull of *Mabel E.Holland* groaned under the crushing pressure of the shifting floes. Experienced ice observers at Resolute had warned me that my effort to get through the Northwest Passage that year was futile and now I was beginning to see that they were right. What had started as a great adventure was threatening to turn into a nightmare; I had challenged the most hostile environment on earth and it was just beginning to give me its reply.

IN THE entire history of exploration, I think it is fair to say that no objective has absorbed more effort, over a longer period, at a greater cost in lives and material, than the search for the Northwest Passage – nor proved as ultimately fruitless. The Norwegian explorer Fridjof Nansen put it succinctly when he wrote 'Nowhere has man moved more slowly, stepped forward with so much trouble, endured so many privations and suffered with the promise of so little material gain.' In spite of this, the lure of the Northwest Passage, the enormous potential benefits that it seemed to offer, plus the extraordinary fascination of the Arctic itself, have always exerted a powerful magnetism on men's minds.

That hard-to-explain attraction certainly held me in its grip, not because I stood to gain from it in any material fashion but simply because the unrealized ambition of a single-handed voyage through the Passage seemed a worthy and ultimately compelling challenge. Although the British had played such an important role in navigating, charting and naming so much of the Arctic; up to 1986 when I began my expedition, no British surface vessel had left from British waters, sailed through the passage and returned. Furthermore no-one of any nationality had made a complete single-handed voyage through the Northwest Passage.

How the Northwest Passage was found, is a tale that would take not just one but many books to tell and we have space here for no more than a quick gallop through the highlights of a long and fascinating piece of history.

It was in 1497 that John Cabot sailed from Bristol in the tiny ship *Mathew* with a crew of 18 men and began more than four centuries of effort to find a northern route from the

Atlantic to the Pacific. He was a Venetian but he had come to England with the idea of selling King Henry VII the proposition that he could sail to 'The Indies' by heading west. In doing this, he was planting seeds in fertile ground because the English king was only too well aware that while Venice held the keys to the overland routes to India and China, Spain had recently taken a giant lead in the journey to the west by sponsoring Christopher Columbus. The latter was not looking for America, of course, but for China which was thought to be the same place as India while the geography of the day was so primitive that it allowed Columbus to believe that The West Indies were islands off the mainland of China.

When Cabot sailed off in the general direction of Newfoundland, he was beginning a process not so much of discovery but rediscovery because he was retracing far earlier voyages by the Vikings and, if Tim Severin is to be believed, St Brendan in his leather curragh. Centuries earlier there had been a thriving Christian community in Greenland who grew crops, raised cattle and whose souls were watched over by a bishop. A worsening of the climate and perhaps the coming of the Black Death killed these communities off but the existence of lands to the west remained a strong folk memory.

By the end of June that year, the little *Mathew* had reached the coast of Newfoundland where Cabot landed briefly and looked around before sailing back to England. Like Columbus, he thought he had found the east coast of India, which is why Europeans henceforth called the inhabitants 'indians', and Cabot suggested to King Henry that he return the following year with a larger and better-equipped expedition. The King was inclined to agree and Cabot set off again in '98 with five ships and the intention of exploring inland. But his little fleet was scattered by an Atlantic gale and only one struggled to safety in an Irish port.

Cabot's son Sebastian established himself as a 'Merchant Adventurer' sailing to various countries out of Bristol and may well have reached Hudson Bay, though this cannot be proved. He claimed he knew how to sail to 'the Indies' but failed to find backers willing to put up the cost of an expedition. In 1527 Henry VIII sent out a couple of ships which achieved nothing and the initial enthusiasm generated by Cabot senior gradually died away.

Instead it fell to the Italian Verrazano to prove that North America was not part of the mainland of Asia. He was sent out by Italian bankers from Lyon in the hope of finding a trade route to the East and instead discovered Long Island Sound. By then stout Cortez had already crossed the Isthmus of Panama and 'gazed with wild surmise on the Pacific' and the penny finally dropped that America was a continent in its own right. However this only increased speculation that there could be 'a way through' to the Indies via some kind of strait or passage to the north.

The initiative then passed to France where François I managed to reach a useful agreement with the Pope which permitted him to claim lands 'Not yet discovered'. This was a way of skirting around the fact that Spain and Portugal already had papal authority to carve up the whole of America between them. François then gave his backing to the tough and experienced sailor Jacques Cartier whom he had met at Mont St Michel. In the following years Cartier undertook three tremendous expeditions which effectively began the exploration of Canada and founded the French colony of Quebec.

On his second voyage in 1535, Cartier sailed up the tidal St Lawrence, a river of such size that you could well believe that it was a strait rather than an estuary, until he reached Quebec. There he transferred to the ship's boats and rowed on to 'Hochelaga', the modern Montreal. However when he came to the Lachine Rapids, Cartier realized that this could not be a navigable route to the Pacific.

In those days, mere information was not thought a sufficient reward for exploration; actual riches were expected, preferably in the form of gold, silver and jewels. The Spanish were already sending home shiploads of loot from Central America so it was perhaps no surprise that on his third voyage Cartier claimed to have found gold and diamonds lying around on the ground. These were in reality iron pyrites and quartz but the rumours spread through the waterfront taverns of Europe like wildfire and set off a new burst of enthusiasm in England.

Only the Elizabethan era, it seems, could produce a character such as Martin Frobisher who combined the roles of pirate, courtier, explorer and merchant with equal distinction. A Yorkshireman, he was twice arrested for piracy and was on the King of Spain's death list before he managed to wangle himself into court circles thanks to the influence of a well-connected girl-friend. He then teamed up with a merchant named Michael Lok who had formed 'The Company of Cathay' with the help of influential investors such as the Earl of Warwick and Lord Treasurer Burghley. Lok made shrewd use of a book written by Sir Humphrey Gilbert entitled 'A Discourse of a Discoverie for a New Passage to Cathia' to persuade investors that a Northwest Passage was out there waiting to be discovered and with money in his pocket was able to fit out an expedition with Frobisher as the leader.

Two tiny ships with 17 crew each and an open pinnace with four aboard, made up Frobisher's fleet for his first voyage in 1576. Not very surprisingly the pinnace never made it and after the two ships reached Greenland the crew of the *Michael* panicked and ran for home. Frobisher was made of sterner stuff and pushed on across Davis Strait until he met the shore of Newfoundland. He then turned north and presently came to the entrance of a great bay or fjord. After he sailed 150 miles down this fjord without reaching the end, he became convinced that it was the sought-after strait. In actual fact it was just one of many such fjords along the coast of Baffin Island that was to prove as deceptive as the 'fool's gold' that he dug up on Hall's Island.

The rock samples with a golden sparkle to them that Frobisher brought home were worthless Marcasite but they enabled the wily Lok to claim that gold had been discovered, bringing a welcome rush of fresh investment. Queen Elizabeth decided to give active support by lending a larger ship, the 200-ton *Aid* which together with *Gabriel* and *Michael* supported a total of 134 men for Frobisher's second expedition in 1577. They had no special equipment other than normal winter clothing but took 80 tuns of beer to sustain them.

This time they failed to land on Greenland due to pack ice but crossed Baffin Bay to Hall's Island were they loaded 20 tons of useless 'ore' from the original source. This time there were skirmishes with the natives, one of whom managed to shoot Frobisher in the backside with an arrow which nevertheless did not prevent him from capturing three natives who were duly taken back to England where they became the object of much curiosity. Lok managed to stall on the subject of the 'gold' by saying that he needed time to find the best way of extracting it from the rock. Meanwhile he was almost trampled to death by the rush of investors and was able to fund a massive expedition of 15 ships for Frobisher's third and final voyage. On this occasion he stumbled on the entrance to Hudson Strait, the most massive fjord of them all and noted a strong east-going current which he suggested (correctly, as it turned out) showed that it must be connected to another ocean. But Frobisher was an opportunist rather than an explorer and did not follow up this vital clue. Instead he filled his ships with tons of useless rock while losing 40 men in fights with the natives.

By the time Frobisher returned to London once again, the bubble had burst. Having failed to extract a single ounce of gold from the previous load of ore, the wretched Lok had been thrown into prison and the rock that had cost so much effort to obtain was eventually used for mending the roads. Finding he was not exactly man of the match, Frobisher returned to his former occupation of piracy. He then joined up with Francis Drake for the latter's piratical attack on the Spanish Main and was knighted after commanding *Triumph* in the battle of the Spanish Armada. True to form to the end, he was killed in a desperate fight with the Spanish at Crozon.

The portrait of Sir Martin Frobisher in the Bodleian Library shows him with one hand on his sword, a pistol in the other and a globe discreetly placed behind his back, which is probably a fair representation of his sense of priorities. Nevertheless he filled in what had been a very large blank space on the chart and almost inadvertently supplied a mass of information about the topography and inhabitants of the region.

The next actor to mount the stage was an entirely different type of person. John Davis was a serious and scholarly professional navigator from Dartmouth who among other things helped to develop the quadrant, ancestor of the modern sextant, which enabled him to fix his latitude reliably. He was backed at first by Sir Humphrey Gilbert, half-brother of Sir Walter Raleigh, and after his death by his brother Adrian. Davis's style could not have been more different from Frobisher's for when he met up with a party of natives on his first voyage to Greenland, instead of manning the guns he sent for the ship's band to strike up a jolly tune. This had the desired effect and Inuk and Englishman were soon exchanging friendly embraces.

One of the great lessons of the Arctic is that the extent of pack-ice varies tremendously from year to year. On his first voyage in 1585, Davis was lucky enough to find the Greenland Coast virtually free of 'Ye pester yce', enabling him to sail north nearly to the Arctic Circle before crossing over to the

Baffin Island side. Here, he found yet another huge fjord (Cumberland Sound) and returned home convinced that it was the Northwest Passage, just as Frobisher had.

But when he returned the following year it was a very different story as massive ice floes blocked the way and the cold and damp affected the men's health so badly that he was forced to send one ship home prematurely. His third voyage in 1587 was the most significant. He reached a headland on the West Greenland shore in 72 degrees 12 minutes North that he named Sanderson's Hope, before crossing over to the Canadian side where he may well have seen Lancaster Sound, the real key to the Northwest Passage. He then turned south and on his way down the coast, passed and correctly fixed the positions, of Cumberland Sound, Frobisher Bay and Hudson Bay though without exploring them. On his return he wrote 'The World's Hydrographical Description' and assisted Emery Molyneaux to create the first English terrestrial globe but the arrival of the Spanish Armada put a stop to his explorations.

Quite separately from these English expeditions, a Spaniard named Juan de Fuca claimed that he had been despatched by the Viceroy of Mexico to find the western end of the Northwest Passage. He coasted his way up the American West Coast until he came to a convincing-looking 'entrance' which was actually Vancouver Sound. The fact that this lies more than 1,000 miles south of the Bering Strait was not so important as the fact that the news eventually trickled back to Europe that the fabled 'Strait of Anian' actually existed and had been found. Never mind that it would have had to be 3,000 miles long and somehow cross the Rocky Mountains! The next real giant of Arctic exploration was Henry Hudson a well-read Londoner who had fallen under the spell of the somewhat dotty Dutch geographer Placius who claimed the North Pole was warm because it received five months of continuous sunshine per year. The ice, he said, was just a rim like a monk's tonsure, concealing an open polar sea. All you had to do was break through the ice barrier before sailing nonchalantly over the North Pole and popping out on the other side of the World. This seductive idea persuaded The Muscovy Company to back Hudson's effort to reach the Pacific by this means.

His effort to sail up the East Coast of Greenland in 1607 was a complete failure so the Company ordered him to direct his efforts to the North-East where the Dutchman Barents had already reached Nova Zemlya. Hudson also reached Nova Zemlya and returned safely with the message that no North-east Passage existed.

The following year, rather strangely, he was commissioned by the Dutch East India Company to sail due north from Nova Zemlya in a further test of the 'Open Polar Sea' hypothesis. The Dutch crew had little stomach for such a crazy voyage and neither had Hudson who promptly turned to the west and sailed right across the North Atlantic to Newfoundland. He then turned south and coasted down past Long Island and up what was later named the Hudson River. Although this was hardly what he had been asked to do, the Dutch got quite good value from a voyage which enabled them to found a settlement known as New Amsterdam and later New York.

The voyage that really interests us was Hudson's fourth and final one which commenced in 1610. Alarmed by the fact that he was working for the Dutch, a City of London syndicate, headed by Sir Dudley Digges, commissioned him to clear up the matter of the Northwest Passage once and for all. Hudson knew where he thought it lay and with a small crew of just 20 men and two boys aboard the *Discovery* went directly to the strait that Frobisher had discovered in 1578. Sailing through it he found to his delight what appeared to be open sea ahead and joyfully turned to the south. Surely, this was it at last – the path to the Strait of Anian. But it was not. Though he had discovered the World's largest enclosed Bay – Hudson Bay – it was a trap that would cost him his life.

Discovery stood on south, hoping to reach warmer latitudes but instead found the land closing in around them as they entered James Bay. It was a dead end, of course, and as it was now too late in the season to retrace their steps they were obliged to overwinter there. Though well south of the Arctic Circle, James Bay has pretty cold winters and Hudson did not have the food or clothing that should have made it a fairly easy stopover. He and his crew were the first to experience the starvation, scurvy and freezing cold that were to become familiar to later explorers. Discipline broke down and Hudson cooked his own goose by demoting some of the most competent members of the crew, including the navigator, Bylot.

Eventually summer returned and the ice began to break up but when Hudson announced that the search for the Northwest Passage would continue, the crew mutinied and cast Hudson, his son and some sick men adrift in a small boat. They were never seen again. The mutineers went ashore to hunt for food but got into a fight with natives during which several of the ringleaders were killed. A pathetic group of nine men struggled back across the Atlantic, so weakened that only Bylot was left standing when they reached Ireland.

Ironically, this harrowing tale only increased interest in the Northwest Passage and set off a fresh burst of activity. Having escaped trial for mutiny, Robert Bylot was drafted to return to the icy north with William Baffin as his pilot. His second voyage in 1616 was the most successful as he managed to sail right round the coast of Baffin Bay (as it was to be named – somewhat unfairly – because Baffin, not Bylot described the voyage) becoming the first to break through into the area of permanently open water or 'polynya' that exists at its northern extremity. No-one sailed further north for another two centuries. But instead of discovering the

Northwest Passage, they found not one but three wide, deep-water sounds, any one of which might have led onwards to the fabled orient.

Smith Sound led due north and separates Greenland from Ellesmere Island while both Jones Sound and Lancaster Sound beckoned westwards. But Baffin and Bylot could only note their position before hurrying on south. The trouble was that in the short time available in one 'sailing season', roughly a month, it was not possible to progress much further than this and still stand a reasonable chance of escaping before winter. The explorers of the day were normal seamen with the ordinary clothing of the period and were totally ill-equipped for an Arctic winter. Those that got caught out and were forced to overwinter such as Jens Munk in 1620 or James in 1631 suffered terribly from scurvy, starvation and frost-bite. Munk, for instance, eventually crawled back to Norway with just three of his crew still alive.

A voyage by Luke Foxe in 1631, during which he cruised around Hudson Bay without finding an exit was the last of that era and brought an end to the 140 year surge of activity. Considering the primitive ships and instruments available to them, these bold sailors of the sixteenth and seventeenth century achieved much but their voyages posed more questions than they answered. Hudson himself wrote the epitaph of the Northwest Passage as a commercial waterway when he said that even if it proved to shorten a passage to the orient by many thousands of leagues, it could hardly reduce the difficulty of the voyage since it was impassable for much of the time.

From the mid-Seventeenth Century therefore, interest in the Northwest Passage waned and even Baffin's discoveries were gradually forgotten until they were finally left off the map. For nearly a hundred years the only Europeans to visit Baffin Bay were whalers and no-one in polite society took them seriously.

Although the French had established the first permanent colony in Canada at Quebec, they did not progress much further west or north, partly because the Iroquois stood in their way. However a couple of tough French 'voyageurs', Medart Chouart, Seieur des Groseilliers (known to the English as Mr Gooseberry) and his brother-in-law Pierre Esprit Radisson (Mr Radish) had penetrated overland to the shores of Hudson Bay and came back with the story that it was a rich source of the furs that were so treasured in Europe. Receiving a frosty reception from the French authorities, they decided to try their luck with the 'rosbifs' and sailed to England where they managed to gain an audience with Charles II.

Charles, who loved anything new and interesting was fascinated by their story and in 1668 sent them off with two ships to trade for furs in Hudson Bay. Rather to everyone's surprise they returned with furs valued at £1,379, a fabulous fortune in the currency of the day. A direct result of this voyage was the founding of the Hudson's Bay Company which was not only of huge value to the City of London, but enabled English traders and colonists to gradually outflank the French as they spread out from their bases on the western shore of Hudson Bay.

In the early years of the 18th Century, a Hudson's Bay employee named James Knight was told by Cree Indians about the Coppermine River which they said positively dripped with precious metals and flowed out into 'The West Sea'. This sounded to Knight like a real bonanza so he rushed home to London convinced that he could find both mineral wealth **and** the Northwest Passage in one shot. He managed to find backers for an expedition consisting of two small ships, *Albany* and *Discovery* manned by 27 men who set off in search of the fabled Coppermine in 1719. And were never seen again. It appears the two vessels were crushed by ice and sank near Marble Island on the western shores of Hudson Bay, another down-payment in the terrible price that the northern regions exacted for their secrets.

The Coppermine River, of course, does exist and does flow out into the Arctic Ocean. The first European to confirm this was the Hudson's Bay employee Samuel Hearne who travelled there overland in the years 1770-2 guided by Chipewyan Indians. Nowadays, there is a growing feeling that 'exploration' in the sense used by Europeans is a patronising term since the whole area was already populated by people who were quite well aware of its geography. The Canadian historian Michael Bliss has voiced the opinion that the 'exploration' of Canada consisted mainly of Europeans being given what amounted to guided tours by the natives.

This is perhaps going a bit far but it is certainly true that more of the geography of Northern Canada was learned from overland expeditions that from ones by sea. Before the end of the 18th Century, Alexander Mackenzie had travelled overland to the Beaufort Sea and the Pacific Coast and had mapped the tremendous river that bears his name. Two epic overland journeys by John Franklin in the early years of the 19th Century charted a thousand miles of the Arctic coastline whereas his seaborne expedition to find the Northwest Passage was the most disastrous and tragic of them all.

What is certainly true of both land and sea expeditions to the North by Europeans is their extraordinary inability to learn the survival techniques of the natives. Europeans died like flies in an area where the natives lived all the year round. For instance it was well-known that scurvy, the debilitating disease that killed many thousands of seamen over the centuries, was caused by lack of fresh food. The Inuit did not suffer from it although they had virtually no access to the fruit or vegetables that were thought to be the most important anti-scorbutics. In fact their survival was due to eating raw meat which contains Vitamin-C. Indeed, the term 'Eskimo' means 'eater of raw meat' a practice that Europeans considered too disgusting to contemplate.

The same was true of clothing and shelter. Europeans would come to the Arctic dressed in wool and leather and attempt to shelter in tents made of canvas, all materials which lost their insulating properties by becoming damp and then freezing. The natives meanwhile kept warm in furs which nature has designed to shed water and wore sealskin 'mukluk' boots insulated with dry grass and moss. While Europeans shivered in their cumbersome tents which were heavy to carry and took ages to pitch, the Inuit were tucked up warmly in their igloos which offered far more protection and could be built in an hour, as and where required.

So far we have been looking at the search for the North-west Passage from a European viewpoint but there was also a vital Asian perspective. When Peter the Great became Tsar of All the Russias, he wanted to know just how far his influence extended and in particular whether Asia really was one seamless landmass extending all the way to the Atlantic. He therefore hired a Dane named Vitus Bering (or Behring) who in 1733 set off from Moscow at the head of a ramshackle army of over 500 cartographers, engineers, academics, cooks and bottle-washers. After sauntering across Siberia for an incredible eight years, Bering eventually reached salt water at Kamchatka. Here, boats were built and an expedition followed the coast north and east until they reached a point from which they could see another shore to the east – Alaska which was duly claimed in the name of the Tsar.

Worn out by his exertions, poor Bering died before he could return and the momentous news of his discovery took a long time to filter back to Europe. Yet the information really was momentous for at last it was known that there was a deep-water strait between Asia and America and that it led into a vast Arctic Ocean. The implication was that if only a way could be found to escape from Baffin Bay, it should be possible to sail right 'over the top' of the American continent and come out into the Pacific via Bering's strait. The Northwest Passage began to beckon once again!

This was at a time in history that British power and influence was beginning to build up an increasing head of steam. Canada was supposed to be coloured red on the Atlas and the idea of the Russians creeping in through the back door was alarming. Up to now, the search for the Northwest Passage had been fuelled by the hope of finding a trade route to the East but now matters of sovereignty and national honour began to enter the picture. Initially, not much was done about it except that the poet Byron's grandfather 'Foulweather Jack' Byron was sent off by the Navy to find the Western exit to the Passage. He failed and so did Captain James Cook, the greatest navigator of the 18th and perhaps any century, who in 1776 sailed up the Pacific coast until he met ice, whereupon he turned round and sailed to the Sandwich Islands (Hawaii) where he met his death in 1779.

More to the point, the Hudson's Bay Company was given orders at the highest level to start taking exploration more seriously. Understandably, it had been reluctant to mount expeditions which held out no commercial advantage but having received an official boot up the rear sent off first Hearne and later Mackenzie to cross the 'barren lands' and investigate the north coast.

The Napoleonic Wars then intervened but had a crucial impact on the story because England emerged from them as the greatest military and commercial power in the World and the one with the largest navy. The trouble was, having won the war they had little left to occupy them. By 1817, 90 percent of British naval officers were unemployed; some 6,000 highly-qualified men with nothing to do except eke out an existence on half pay. One of the men responsible for finding them something to do was John Barrow, Second Secretary of the Admiralty.

The catalyst for a new wave of exploration was a whaling Captain named William Scoresby who in 1817 wrote to Sir Joseph Banks, the most famous naturalist of the age, to say that ice conditions on the Greenland Coast were the best in anyone's memory. The sea was 'perfectly devoid of ice' as far as 80 degrees North, he said. This Scoresby was a remarkable man who spent the summers whaling and the winters studying at Edinburgh University. He was a meticulous observer who probably knew more about the Arctic than any other European at that time.

Banks was nearing the end of his life but still had a lot of influence and at his suggestion, the Royal Society persuaded Parliament to offer very substantial cash prizes to anyone who could unlock the secret of the Northwest Passage. This went in stages: £5,000 for the first person (they meant first Englishman, of course) to reach 110 degrees West, £10,000 for reaching 130 West, £15,000 for 150 West and £20,000 for getting right through to the Pacific. Very big money in those days!

Banks also spoke to Barrow and commended the exploration of the North as a fit objective for the Royal Navy. He even suggested a naval expedition with Scoresby as its commander! This idea of putting a mere whaler in charge of naval officers went down like a lead balloon with Barrow but he seized on the idea of a naval expedition with enthusiasm. He has been called the father of modern Arctic exploration in spite of the fact that he personally never ventured further north than Yorkshire. What Barrow did was unleash the full strength of the Royal Navy onto solving the problem of the Northwest Passage. In fact it became an obsession with him, and expedition after expedition was sent off even when it was clear to all that the Passage had no possible commercial or military significance. This was the age of discovery, of scientific enquiry and exploration of every kind. It was also the age of Empire when there was nothing, absolutely nothing, that could not be achieved by a British officer at the head of properly trained and equipped men.

First away was Commander John Ross a red-haired Scot with an outstanding war record who was put in command of two chartered whaling ships, *Isabella* and *Alexander* with civilian crews and another naval officer, Lt William Parry as second in command. They set off in the Spring of 1818 and their first shock was to find that the ice had returned to Baffin Bay. In fact, there had just been an exceptionally cold winter and the large whaling fleet they met up with off the Greenland Coast was having difficulty in breaking through into the 'North Water'.

Officially, Baffin Bay did not exist. For some reason Barrow had decided that it was all a fiction and he also maintained an irrational belief in Placius' crazy notion of the 'Open Polar Sea'. Ross and Parry soon found that Baffin Bay was no fiction and in fact Baffin's two hundred year-old chart was pretty accurate. They landed and met up with a very remote colony of Inuit at Etah at the entrance to Smith Sound, the scene being recorded in a drawing done by their Greenland interpreter John Sacheuse. As well as being one of the great masterpieces of naive art, this picture shows a fascinating meeting between two totally different cultures. Ross and Parry are standing on the ice in full naval uniform, including swords and tricorn hats while the natives are dressed in furs and are staring with horror at their own reflections in a mirror that they have just been given.

Anyway, that was a bit of a diversion but the next thing to happen caused one of the greatest controversies in the whole era of 19th Century exploration. The *Isabella* and *Alexander* next sailed round past Smith Sound to Lancaster Sound where they found the expected open water and this magnificent, broad waterway nearly 80 miles wide, heading due west. Ross's ship was faster and went ahead and after being in the fog that is so common in the area for a while, he was called by the officer of the watch to say that the visibility had cleared. Clapping his telescope to his eye, Ross immediately declared that he could see a range of mountains barring the way ahead and ordered the ship to be put about.

Following astern, Parry was astonished to find the flagship coming back under full sail. He could not see any mountains and nor could any of his crew. Anyway, the expedition retreated and sailed straight back to England. Barrow was furious and virtually accused Ross of cowardice. Parry said little because he had his eye on the main chance – command of a new expedition.

In this he was successful, as in so many things. Parry was a man we might typify today as a 'public school type' though in actual fact he had joined the navy at the age of 12; well-educated, from a good family, confident and competent at everything he tackled and with strong Christian values. Having sailed with Ross, he knew more about the Arctic than anyone else in the Navy and as a result his preparations were the most thorough and thoughtful ever undertaken. He took lemon juice, pickles and sauerkraut as anti-scorbutics and a large amount of tinned food – a new invention. He fully expected to spend at least one winter in the Arctic and stocked up with books, music, games and everything else he could think of to keep the crews amused during the winter months. The ships he was given, *Hecla* and *Griper* were a lot more suitable than the previous two.

He also chose a remarkably young crew: other than the scientific officer Sabine who had also sailed with Ross, Parry was the oldest officer at 28. The others, including Ross's nephew James Clark Ross were all in their early twenties. They all worshipped Parry and would have followed him to hell. Not that he was going in that direction. On the contrary, he knew exactly where he was going: straight to Lancaster Sound.

In fact his biggest mistake was that he tried to go too straight as it was still not fully understood that to cross Baffin Bay, you must go right around its perimeter. Parry tried to batter his way across the middle and had to retreat and then try again further north. Nevertheless by July 28, 1819 the two ships broke through into open water and Lancaster Sound stood before them. Without the slightest hesitation, Parry led the way straight down it. As well as being resolute he was lucky because it was a good year and the two ships sailed almost the whole length of rugged Devon Island before meeting ice.

On their left, Prince Regent Inlet opened up; another huge sound 40 miles across, so they turned into it and sailed south for more than one hundred miles before ice barred the way again. Parry was beginning to realize this was not so much a channel as an archipelago of large islands and that his task was to find the correct path between them.

Retracing their wakes to Lancaster Sound once more, the two ships were turned again to the West, this time finding open water along the Devon Island coast. On and on they sailed past more large islands that they named Cornwallis and Bathhurst. By 4 September Parry was able to tell his crew that they had passed longitude 110 degrees west and won £5,000. Eventually the weather broke and they were forced to seek shelter in a small bay on Melville Island that they christened Winter Harbour, a full 700 miles west of the entrance to Lancaster Sound.

It had been a tremendous achievement but Parry's leadership during the winter months was just as praiseworthy. His idea was to keep everyone too busy to become bored. The ships had their decks roofed over with canvas, giving protection from the wind and keeping the decks clear of snow. Every day was filled with a full schedule of cleaning, exercise and shipboard work. Strict attention was paid to diet and personal hygiene. During free time, concerts and plays were arranged and a ship's newspaper was produced.

In the years that followed, many poked fun at Parry and his concert-party antics but the fact is that not only was his expedition the first to survive for a whole winter north of the Arctic circle but only one man from the whole expedition died. Meanwhile he had charted and named a vast selection of inlets, bays, points, headlands, straits and sounds.

The following year was a great disappointment for Parry had been sure they were going to go crashing through to the Bering Strait. In fact they only got a few miles further west before heavy pack blocked their way. By climbing a nearby mountain, they could see further high land about fifty miles to the west (Banks Land) and they could also see that the ice was solid all the way. This was the real polar pack ice and there was no chance that a sailing ship would ever penetrate it. There was no alternative but to turn round and head back east. By October 1820 he was back in London, justly hailed as a hero. His report to Barrow confirmed a) that the Northwest Passage undoubtedly existed but that b) the route he had followed was not a practical one.

At the same time as Parry was battering his way down Barrow Strait, another naval officer John Franklin was walking to the mouth of the Coppermine River whence he canoed 500 miles eastward along the coast before returning, with the utmost difficulty, to Hudson Bay. Five years later he set off again on a much more ambitious overland trip to the mouth of the Mackenzie. This time walking westward along the coast, he *almost* met up with HMS *Blossom* (Captain Beechey) which was the first British vessel to sail into the Arctic Sea via the Bering Strait. Quite logically, Barrow was chipping away at the unknown territory from both ends, confident that his naval explorers would eventually meet in the middle.

Parry's next expedition was to Hudson Bay because it was still believed that this contained a secret exit. This he found to

Parry's next expedition was to Hudson Bay because it was still believed that this contained a secret exit. This he found to be true: at the very top left-hand corner of Hudson Bay, a narrow strait that he named *Fury* and *Hecla* Strait, leads out into Prince Regent Inlet but it was permanently beset by ice and he never managed to penetrate it. The only worthwhile outcome of an incredibly arduous expedition lasting 27 months was the extended contact with the natives at the settlement of Igloolik which led to a far better understanding of their way of life.

His third and final sea expedition was once again via Lancaster Sound but this time turning south into Prince Regent Inlet. In an exceptionally bad season, he failed to find the 'back-door' from that inlet, Bellot Strait, and the faithful *Fury* was wrecked though all her crew were rescued and taken home by *Hecla*. Both these expeditions were great disappointments compared to his first. Though it forms no part of the Northwest Passage story, Parry later went on to make an epic sledge journey from Spitzbergen towards the North Pole during which he reached a latitude of 82 degrees 45 minutes north, an achievement not bettered for another 50 years.

Stung by being considered faint-hearted, John Ross was determined to have another go and managed to find sponsorship from the gin distiller Felix Booth. In 1829 he set off in a wonky paddle steamer named *Victory* that had been the former Isle of Man ferry. In this totally unsuitable vessel he and his crew chugged down Prince Regent Inlet without finding Bellot Strait and got stuck there for an incredible *three years*. They then walked overland to Fury Beach where they were forced to spend another winter sustained by the supplies salvaged from the *Fury* wreck. The following summer they sailed out to Lancaster Sound in *Fury*'s small boats and by an incredible coincidence met up with the whaler *Isabella* which Ross had commanded on his first expedition.

The whole expedition was a disaster but not a complete one. Ross's energetic nephew James Clark Ross made some long sledge journeys during which he crossed right over the Boothia Peninsular, found the site of the Magnetic North Pole (at the time) and crossed over the next bit of sea to King William Island. Meanwhile Uncle James, though unpopular with his men, forced them to eat Inuit food because he realized, at last, that it must be their diet that protected them from scurvy. The Inuit showed them how to hunt and fish and saved their lives. It was an epic of hard-won knowledge.

Ten years later Barrow, now aged 80 and on the point of retirement, was ready for the final push. In the interim, two important land expeditions had filled in a lot more of the map. Back and King had followed the Great Fish River to its mouth to the west of the Boothia Peninsular, having been sent out to find what had happened to the Rosses. Meanwhile the Hudson's Bay Company had commissioned two major expeditions by Peter Dease and Thomas Simpson, each of which commenced by following the Mackenzie down to the Arctic Coast. On the first occasion they turned left and travelled the whole way to Point Barrow, the north-west 'corner' of Alaska. On the second, they made a remarkable small-boat journey eastward along the coast from the Mackenzie as far as Rae Strait.

Between them, these three expeditions succeeded in completing the map of the Arctic coastline apart from the short section from Rae Strait to Boothia Peninsular and, as the acerbic Dr Richard King pointed out, if mapping were the main concern, it could be completed far more readily and cheaply by overland expeditions than by sea voyages. This opinion did not cut any ice with Secretary Barrow who still nurtured the dream of naval ships triumphantly crunching their way through to the Pacific.

Almost every feature of the Admiralty's 1845 expedition was 'over the top'. The two ships selected, *Erebus* and *Terror* were too big and clumsy and, with a draught of 19 feet, incapable of using the inshore leads that are often the only way of making progress in the Arctic. The vast crew of 129 men meant that an enormous volume of stores were needed and that there was little chance of living off the country with so many mouths to feed. Primitive steam engines had been fitted to the ships with the result that much space had to be devoted to the bunkering of coal.

Sir John Franklin was a veteran explorer, with the emphasis on 'veteran'. Following an unsatisfactory period as Governor of Van Dieman's Land, Franklin had an intense desire to round off his career with a big success but at 59 years old and after a long and arduous career he was not particularly fit. Barrow's orders to Franklin were that he should sail directly down Lancaster Sound and Barrow Strait and only turn to the north or south if unable to make progress straight ahead. This really defied the evidence of Parry and others that once out of the shelter of the islands, the ships would meet impenetrable polar pack-ice. The ships were provisioned for three years but remarkably, there seems to have been no understanding of what was supposed to happen if they did not turn up after this time. Incredibly, there was no formal arrangement for leaving messages at various points, so that they could, if necessary be followed. Apparently, the possibility of failure was not considered.

Without becoming too bogged down in an immensely complex story, the Franklin Expedition sailed off into the Arctic and disappeared. For two years the Admiralty did exactly nothing and it was not until 1848 that three relief expeditions were organized. James Clark Ross (by now Sir James) was to follow Franklin's anticipated track by ship. Capt. Henry Kellett was to approach from the other direction via the Bering Strait while Sir John Richardson and Dr John Rae were to walk down the Mackenzie and search eastward from there.

23

As usual the man nearest the mark was Dr King who proposed a land expedition down the Great Fish River. With the benefit of hindsight we can say that such an expedition should have found Franklin's ships which were trapped in the area to the west of the Boothia Peninsular, near the northern tip of King William Island but King was so heartily disliked by the Admiralty that they ignored him. Neither of the sea-borne expeditions found anything but Dr Rae came within about 50 miles of where Franklin's ships lay trapped.

A public outcry in England, skilfully orchestrated by Lady Jane Franklin, led to more and more rescue expeditions being sent out in the following years, none of which succeeded. However the greatest irony of the Northwest Passage story lies in the fact that the final pieces of the Arctic jigsaw were filled in as a result of the long drawn-out search for Franklin. We must confine ourselves to looking briefly at two of them, those of McClure and M'Clintock. Both men served as lieutenants on Sir James Clark Ross's 1848 expedition and knew their stuff but were very different characters.

Robert McClure was something of a maverick character. With an Eton and Sandhurst background he swapped from Army to Navy aged 17 and was incredibly ambitious. Tough, moody, short-tempered and difficulty to get along with, he took appalling risks with his own and other men's lives in his efforts to win fame and fortune.

His position in 1850 was actually subordinate to Capt. Richard Collinson who commanded a two-ship expedition consisting of the ships *Investigator* and *Enterprise*, their three-year mission, to boldly go into the Arctic sea via the Bering Strait and search eastward for the Franklin Expedition which had by then been missing for five years. The two ships were supposed to sail independently and rendezvous at Bering Strait but McClure got there first by taking a risky short cut through the Aleutian Islands and then deliberately disobeyed his orders by going ahead without waiting for Collinson. He

24

had some justification in this because Collinson was an incredibly cautious fellow who eventually returned to England with most of his officers under arrest because he had driven them mad by his lack of action. It was obvious, however, that McClure was not so much interested in finding poor old Franklin as finding the Northwest Passage and collecting the famous prize.

Off went the *Investigator* at a cracking pace along the north shore of Alaska. On one occasion when ice barred the way McClure set full sail and rammed straight into the barrier which miraculously cracked and let the ship through. When it was calm, he had nearly the whole crew out in the boats, working like galley-slaves to tow the ship. By early August he reached the eastern side of Banks Island which had been seen from the opposite direction by Parry 30 years earlier. He was within 150 miles of completing the Northwest Passage.

McClure's error was in not sticking to the mainland shore. Like so many others he did not fully appreciate that the main obstacle was the steady drift of heavy polar pack-ice from the Northwest. This vast, slow-moving ice-sheet is up to 30ft thick and piles up into even thicker pressure ridges when it meets an obstruction. There is no way that a sailing ship could ever penetrate it. The only way to make progress is by following shore leads or by staying in the lee of islands that offer protection from the ice-stream.

Finding his onward passage blocked, McClure followed a lead to the north which led him into the narrow passage between Banks Island and Victoria Island and very nearly managed to pop out the other end into Viscount Melville Sound. At this point he was less than 100 miles from Parry's 'Winter Harbour' and tantalizingly close to making the final link-up before being driven back by moving ice which nearly smashed the ship. Before this happened, he walked to the outlet of the Strait and from a hill-top looked out over open water to Melville Island in the distance. Beyond a shadow of doubt, the Northwest Passage existed!

After surviving the winter, McClure retreated from the narrow strait (Prince of Wales Strait) but then made the fatal mistake of trying to sail around the north coast of Banks Island instead of going back to the mainland. Following a shore lead so narrow that the crew had to use gunpowder to blast away pieces of overhanging rock, the battered *Investigator* crept right round the island until she nearly reached the exit to Prince of Wales Strait again. But then McClure finally seemed to lose his nerve and on reaching a protective inlet he named Mercy Bay, put the ship into winter quarters once more. And there she remained for the next two years.

The Arctic was beginning to act like fly-paper. Having lost one entire expedition, the Navy sent out others which also got stuck. At one stage ten British and American ships were locked in the unheeding ice. If only McClure had not been so impetuous he could have gone back on foot to Collinson's *Enterprise* which was less than 150 miles behind. Or he could have travelled east across the ice and met up with the various search-parties in the Barrow Strait area. He did neither, and when he finally got round to making a sledge journey to Winter Harbour he found a message left there the previous June by M'Clintock which implied that by then the search would have been called off and everyone but his own crew on their way home.

That the crew of *Investigator* was not added to the death-toll of the Franklin expedition was thanks mainly to the father of her Second Officer, one Samuel Gurney Cresswell, a grandson of the prison reformer Elizabeth Fry, who kept badgering the Admiralty to do something. In this he was eventually successful and in 1852 the Navy sent out to the Eastern Arctic a five-ship last-ditch effort to find either Franklin or McClure. By the spring of 1853 McClure's crew were at the end of their tether, suffering terribly from starvation, scurvy and mental illness after being cooped up for three years.

Luckily for McClure and his men, one of the five relief ships was commanded by the immensely sensible Henry Kellett who had with him M'Clintock and an eccentric loner named Bedford Pim, one of life's natural wanderers who had seriously proposed walking across Siberia in search of Franklin. Battering west as far as Dealy Island, Kellett sent sledge parties fanning out ahead, one of which found McClure's note at Winter Harbour. Now they knew where *Investigator* lay and Pim volunteered to go and find her, setting off with a small sledge party in March 1853. He understood the value of travelling light and soon abandoned the cumbersome man-hauled sledge he had been issued with, carrying on with just two men and a dog-sled. Even M'Clintock, considered the best sledge man in the Navy, did not use dogs. A month later he found *Investigator* just in time as her miserable, half-dead crew prepared for a suicidal attempt to walk to the Mackenzie River.

Instead of mustering his whole crew for the relatively short journey to Dealy Island and safety, McClure returned with Pim alone for the incredible reason that he wanted to persuade Kellett to re-supply him so that he could continue his efforts to sail through the Northwest Passage. Fortunately, Kellett had more sense and sent his doctor to check the condition of *Investigator*'s crew with the authority to order McClure to abandon the ship and walk his crew out. Three of them died while he was away but the remainder tottered across the ice to Dealy Island. In so doing they became the first to complete the Northwest Passage – but they did it on foot!

By 1854 the Admiralty was fed up with the Arctic. Barrow had gone and too many good men and expensive ships had been lost. In any case, the Crimean War had broken out and The Navy no longer needed an adventure playground to keep its officers out of mischief. As far as they were concerned there was no longer any mystery about the Northwest Passage and there was not the slightest chance that any member of the Franklin expedition could be alive. The only person still in the fight was Lady Jane Franklin who was determined to find out what had happened to her husband, even if it took her last penny.

The first real information came from Dr John Rae who was not even looking for Franklin but set off in 1853 on a more-or-less routine survey expedition. In April 1854, while at Pelly Bay, at the bottom of the Gulf of Boothia, he met some natives, one of whom was wearing a naval cap-band which he said had come from a white man who had died near a river to the west. Recognizing that this could have been one of Franklin's men, Rae said he would pay for any other relics and was soon rewarded with a considerable collection of buttons, badges, silver spoons and the like which without any doubt linked them to the Franklin expedition. He hurried to England, arriving in September 1854 at about the same time as Belcher, Kellett, McClure, M'Clintock and their crews.

The information that Rae brought back was enough for the Admiralty but not for Jane Franklin who kept battering away at them and finally, when it was clear that their Lordships would not commit any more ships and men to the search, decided to pay for an expedition herself. To this end she personally bought the 177 ton schooner-rigged steam yacht *Fox* and offered her command to Leopold M'Clintock who accepted, without pay. In fact all the officers were unpaid volunteers and when *Fox* sailed from Aberdeen in 1857, it was not under the white ensign of the Royal Navy but the defaced blue of the Royal Harwich Yacht Club. She was a far smaller vessel than the Navy's deep-draught sailing ships but man-oeuvrable and able to sail into shallow water.

One season was wasted because she got stuck in Baffin Bay but in '58 *Fox* reached Beechey Island where her bunkers were refilled with coal from stocks left there by previous naval expeditions. Thanks to Rae, M'Clintock knew he must head south and thanks to Kennedy and Bellot, officers who had been involved in the Franklin search, he knew there was a way through from the East to the West side of the Boothia Peninsular, the Bellot Strait. Finding Peel Sound too heavily iced he therefore made his way down Prince Regent Inlet, past the dreaded *Fury* Beach, and on to Bellot Strait. Six times he tried to force the reluctant *Fox* through the narrow strait, each time being pushed back by a combination of ice and the strong tidal stream, which runs at up to eight knots.

Eventually, M'Clintock gave up and prepared to over-winter at the eastern end of Bellot, which he christened Port Kennedy. As well as being one of the most experienced Arctic navigators alive, M'Clintock was the most rational and stable and also the Navy's the greatest expert in sledging. He himself still believed in man-hauled sledges for carrying heavy weight but accepted that lightweight dog-teams were a lot faster and had a team of 22 dogs with an experienced driver, Carl Petersen.

As soon as *Fox* was frozen in, M'Clintock and Petersen set off on a lightning sledge journey that covered more than 400 miles and filled in the remaining small gap in the chart of the Boothian coastline. He at last found that King William *land* was actually King William *Island* and he was convinced that the solution to the Franklin mystery would be found on its western shore.

Early next spring, as soon as the days were light enough, he and his lieutenants, Allen Young and William Hobson set off in different directions on carefully pre-planned sledging trips around King William Island and the estuary of the Great Fish River. Like Rae, they asked any Inuit they met to bring them 'white men's goods' and were soon rewarded with a mountain of trinkets but it fell to Hobson to find the one piece of paper that told the story of the Franklin expedition.

On a naval form hidden in a stone cairn there were two messages. The first, written in May 1847 said that all was well with the crews of *Erebus* and *Terror*. During the previous year they had sailed right round Cornwallis Island before heading south down Peel Sound towards King William Island. The second message was dated two years later and signed by Franklin's deputies Crozier and James. This revealed that the two ships had been stuck in the ice for the previous 19 months and that Franklin had died in June 1847. At the time the note was written, nine officers and 15 men had died and the remainder had abandoned their ships and were trying to make their way south to the Great Fish River.

This course of action was irrational as help, if it came, would arrive from the north and there was no way the weakened survivors could have struggled a thousand miles across the barren tundra to Hudson Bay. M'Clintock himself found even more striking and pathetic evidence that the Franklin survivors had lost their senses when he came across, first a 28ft whaler and later a massive sledge, complete with human skeletons. Both were absolutely loaded down with a mountain of useless junk such as silver cutlery, books, tooth-brushes, sea-boots, cigar-cases and the like. A small army of fit men could not have dragged such a load right across King William Island, let alone a ragged band of starved and weakened invalids.

One solution to the mystery of why Franklin's crew acted as they did was offered by Dr Owen Beattie, Professor of Anthropology at the University of Alberta. It has been known for some years that three of Franklin's men died during their first winter and were buried on Beechey Island. In 1984 Beattie got permission from the Canadian Government to exhume these bodies and subject them to post-mortem examination. Because they had been buried in permanently-frozen ground, the corpses were perfectly preserved. Beattie's book describing this operation (*Frozen in Time* by Owen Beattie and John Geiger, Grafton Books 1987) makes fascinating but grim reading while the photographs are definitely not recommended for anyone with a weak stomach.

The three men had died for different reasons but the linking factor was that they were all suffering from a degree of lead poisoning. Beattie concludes that this had come from the tinned food which was a major part of the expedition's diet. The hand-made tins were closed with lead solder which apparently leached into the contents. A characteristic of lead poisoning is loss of mental function. So it seems that after a couple of years, poor old Franklin and his crew were suffering from a dreadful mixture of scurvy and lead poisoning, apart from the rigours of the Arctic and the dangers of the pack-ice. Ironically, they had been on the right track but for the relatively small mistake of going the wrong side of King William Island, though whether their clumsy ships could have got through the narrow channels to the south of it is another question.

M'Clintock's expedition established what had happened to Franklin and at the same time, filled in the last remaining blank spots on the chart. So ended the Victorian era of British Naval exploration, with a mixture of tragedy and triumph. Not one ship had managed to get through from Atlantic to Pacific, or *vice versa* but in failing to do so, the entire Arctic coastline had been charted. It was a very costly survey.

Key to whole NW Passage route

1 Banks Island
2 Melville Island
3 Resolute on Cornwallis Island
4 Somerset Island (Fort Ross at S. tip)
5 Bellot Strait

6 Boothia Peninsula
7 King William Island (including Gjoa Haven)
8 Devon Island
9 Lancaster Sound
10 Ellesmere Island

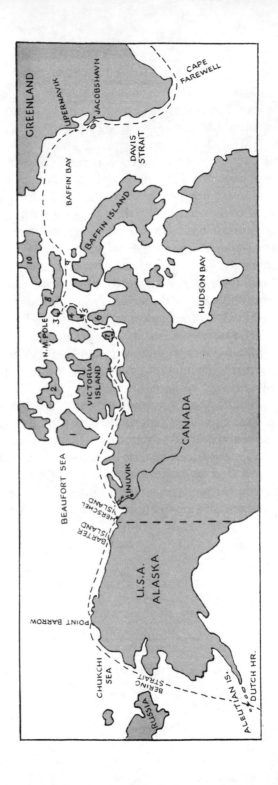

Chapter 2
The final link

WHEN the Franklin search wound down, it brought the heroic era of British naval exploration of the Arctic to a close. Henceforth there were some private expeditions such as that of Sir Allen Young, who had sailed with M'Clintock and had another shot in 1875 in his yacht *Pandora*, and there were an increasing number of overland expeditions. Although the possibility of sailing through by water was still tantalising, the geography of the area was now pretty well-known and there was really no need to hurl vast resources into further exploration. In any case, the Northwest Passage was beginning to be forgotten as the big prize was by then the North Pole.

Not everyone forgot the Northwest Passage however. For a young Norwegian named Roald Amundsen it became an obsession. Oddly enough it was Franklin's published account of his harrowing overland expeditions to the Mackenzie river, which Amundsen read when he was fifteen, that inspired him. Subsequently he collected and read every single account of every arctic expedition there had ever been. Through these, he familiarized himself with all the problems that these expeditions had faced. Health, navigation, types of food, different types of ship, clothing; whatever the subject, the young Amundsen knew all about it.

Nor did he neglect his own personal development. While still at school he took every opportunity to toughen himself up, especially with skiing and climbing expeditions in the winter. As soon as he was old enough, he joined an arctic sealing vessel as an ordinary seaman, meanwhile studying for his officer's ticket and as soon as he had got that he joined a Belgian antarctic expedition as Mate. This gave him enough sea time to qualify for a Master's ticket at the remarkably young age of eighteen.

The key thing about Amundsen was that he wanted to be completely competent in every skill that was relevant to arctic navigation. In this way he could avoid having to rely on the skills of others and could keep his expedition small. Recognising that merely sailing through the Northwest Passage was no longer enough, he decided that his expedition would have a scientific basis and went to Hamburg to study under the leading expert of the day in terrestrial magnetism. The matter to be studied was the nature of the magnetic north pole. Where was it? Did it remain fixed or did it move about and if so was there a discernable pattern? In an era when the magnetic compass was the single most important navigational instrument, this was highly relevant information to seafarers everywhere. He also travelled to England to meet as many of the old explorers as were still alive, calling on Sir Allen Young, Sir Clements Markham and Sir Leopold M'Clintock.

If Amundsen is beginning to sound like a paragon, it should be pointed out that he was hopeless with money. Though he called on all manner of Government bodies and scientific institutions he never managed to raise any worthwhile amount of sponsorship and is alleged to have finally sailed from Oslo at midnight in order to give his creditors the slip. He borrowed money from his brother to buy his expedition vessel, the 22m (72ft) *Gjöa* which was already 30 years old, just as *Mabel E.Holland* was when I bought her! Although registered as a yacht, *Gjöa* had been built as a sturdy coastal fishing vessel and could be called a motor-sailer as she had a small motor in addition to her sails. Her small size ensured that the expedition consisted of just seven men including Amundsen himself but this was as he intended. Patience and a small vessel would succeed where big ships and brute force had failed, he believed. She must have been absolutely jammed tight with stores as they reckoned to be able to survive for up to five years.

Setting off from Oslo in June 1903, Amundsen and his six companions made good time to Baffin Bay and thence to Lancaster Sound. It was soon clear that he had struck one of those lucky years when the sea was comparatively open and *Gjöa* reached Beechey Island on 22 August with relatively few problems. She then set off down Peel Sound towards the most difficult part of the passage. Thanks mainly to his fellow-countryman Fridtjof Nansen's extraordinary drift across the polar ice-cap in *Fram*, Amundsen knew that the real barrier to navigation in that area was caused by the constant slow movement of polar pack-ice from the north-west and that the way to beat it was to stay, as far as possible, in the shelter of islands.

To begin with therefore, Amundsen could take advantage of the shelter of Prince of Wales Island to take him down as far as Bellot Strait and here he was certainly fortunate in finding open water in the area where M'Clintock had waited for two years without being able to move, where Allen Young had been forced to turn back and where I was to come to a standstill so many years later. Things became tougher when he tackled the lengthy exposed section between Prince of Wales Island and King William Island. Forced to sail along an increasingly narrow shore lead, *Gjöa* went aground on a reef.

The crew jettisoned deck cargo in an effort to lighten her but without success. Finally, a gale began to blow and in a desperate gamble Amundsen set full sail and the long-suffering *Gjöa* bounced across the rocks into deep water. It was a story that could so easily have had a different ending. Thanks to the surveys by M'Clintock and others, Amundsen knew what Franklin had not known; that King William *Land* was in fact King William *Island* and *Gjöa* now entered the strait between it and the Boothia Peninsular that had never previously been navigated. Amundsen found it to be a shallow, rocky archipelago leading him to doubt whether Franklin's big ships could ever have got through, even had they known about it. Pushing on to the south-eastern corner of the island, Amundsen came across what his crew described as 'The finest little harbour in the world' and although open water beckoned to the west, he decided to call a halt at the place he named *Gjöa Haven*.

Here he set up huts ashore and constructed a magnetic observatory. Soon he was visited by an entire tribe of Netsilik Inuit who, almost incredibly, gave him a clear account of the visit to the North Magnetic Pole of James Clark Ross, 75 years earlier! With the assistance of the Netsilik, Amundsen's small crew were able to live off the land and passed the winter with remarkably little trouble and no illness. The following season, they made no effort to move on as they wished to survey the area and, in particular to visit the North Magnetic Pole then situated about 90 miles north of their encampment. By finding the cairn built 75 years previously by James Clark Ross, Amundsen discovered that the magnetic pole had indeed moved about 30 miles meanwhile. Since then, incidentally, the wandering magnetic pole has moved about 200 miles further north.

Just as important to Amundsen was the immense amount he learned from the Inuit during his protracted stay. He and his crew 'went native' with enthusiasm and gained a full understanding of Inuit survival methods and particularly of their extremely efficient clothing. This knowledge was to prove a crucial advantage a few years later when he made his famous dash to the South Pole while Robert Falcon Scott was engaged on his death march using outdated British naval clothing and methods.

In August 1905, Amundsen was ready to move, and, as the ice broke up, sailed out into the shallow, shoal-girt waters of Simpson Strait. In just one week he reached Cambridge Bay, where Collinson had wintered so many years before, and in so doing forged the last remaining link in the Northwest Passage. Ironically, it turned out that only about 150 miles had separated Franklin's furthest West from Collinson's furthest East.

From this point on, Amundsen was in charted waters and was able to make good progress until, shortly before the end of August they met a San Francisco whaler, the *Charles Hepson* whose crew knew about *Gjöa* and her crew and warmly congratulated them on being the first to make it through the Northwest Passage. Actually, this was a little premature as, in company with several other whalers, they failed to extricate themselves in time and got stuck near Herschel Island. Being impatient to tell the world of his success, Amundsen then made an overland trek to Eagle, on the Yukon River, where there was a telegraph station. Thanks to the Klondike Gold Rush this was now an outpost of civilization.

Not till the following September, 1906, did the gallant little *Gjöa* finally sail into Nome, Alaska to a huge welcome and world-wide publicity. One of her crew had died of pneumonia during the final winter but the others were positively hale and healthy thanks to their careful preparation and adoption of an Inuit diet. It had been a fantastic achievement by a low-budget expedition, bringing to a conclusion four centuries of effort to penetrate the Northwest Passage. Detractors of Amundsen said he had merely scaled the ladder that others had set up. This is nonsense; he had dedicated his whole life up to this point to this single objective and only succeeded because he devoted so much time to analysing where all the previous attempts had gone wrong.

One thing that Amundsen's three-year voyage had made perfectly clear was that the Northwest Passage was not, nor could it ever be, a practical trade route. Not that this stopped people from flying in the face of this conclusion, right up to the present day.

However there are many more reasons for visiting the Arctic: research, hunting for oil or minerals, tourism or politics. Yes, politics! Since the beginning of this century there has been a long-running dispute between Canada and the United States over the ownership of the Northwest Passage. Most of the islands were claimed by British naval officers (ignoring the rights of the people who already lived there) who claimed them for the Crown. In turn these proprietary rights were vested in the Dominion of Canada which nowadays claims as Canadian territory the whole of the area up to the Arctic Ocean, except, of course for Alaska. The United States, on the other hand, regards the Northwest Passage as part of the ocean and legally as international waters and a niggling dispute about this has gone on for years. The need to establish sovereignty is one reason why outposts such as Resolute are maintained by the Canadian Government.

This squabble threatened to break out into a serious dispute in 1969 when the international oil companies were considering how to transport the newly-discovered supply from the North Slope of Alaska to refineries in the south. One idea was to use special ice-breaking tankers capable of cutting their way through the Northwest Passage to the US East Coast or through the Bering Strait to the West.

To test this idea, the Esso company actually commissioned and built a fantastic ice-strengthened super-tanker, the 155,000 ton *Manhattan* which made a trial voyage in August 1969, accompanied by US and Canadian icebreakers. The intention was to batter straight through Lancaster Sound, Parry Channel and McClure Strait so as to avoid all tricky navigation between islands but although this amazing vessel could call on steam turbines of 42,000 horsepower, the polar pack-ice eventually brought her to a standstill and she was holed several times. With difficulty, she was extricated and turned south for the more sheltered waters of Prince of Wales Strait. By this means she reached Prudhoe Bay where she loaded a single symbolic barrel of oil before retracing her course.

The enormous cost of the special ship, and the fact that she had only just got through with the help of icebreakers, made it clear that shipping oil in this way was not a practical proposition, especially on a year-round basis. The project was therefore abandoned and instead the oil companies jointly paid for the overland pipeline to Valdez on the southern coast of Alaska which can be reached by ships throughout the year. In many ways it is a relief that the Northwest Passage did not become a shipping highway because pollution would have been virtually inevitable in the long term, as the *Exxon Valdez* disaster has shown. As it is, the continuing oil search in the area has brought 'civilization' to the Arctic and changed the way of life of the people living there for ever. Canada and the US agreed to differ on whether the Northwest Passage is coastal or part of international waters.

The first yachtsman, and very nearly the first *solo* yachtsman to transit the Northwest Passage was the Dutchman Willy de Roos in 1977. An extremely experienced sailor who had already made many long single-handed passages, Willy decided to have a crack at the Northwest Passage after selling his garage business in Belgium. His yacht *Williwaw* was a sturdy steel auxiliary ketch 13m (42ft 7in)in length with a 62hp Thornycroft diesel engine. An engineer by profession, de Roos took great care in the preparation of the boat including the addition of a sloping false bow which he hoped would help the yacht ride up over the ice like an ice-breaker. The yacht was planned for single-handed sailing and was fitted with a Decca autopilot and an auxiliary generator, in addition to the main engine. In the cabin was a diesel-fired heating stove which proved to be worth its weight in gold.

Although Willy had often sailed *Williwaw* single-handed, he had second thoughts when he reached Greenland because he doubted if he was up to the physical strain involved in sailing through ice. He therefore telephoned a young Belgian who had already been to the Arctic on a scientific expedition and asked him to fly out and join him. But although Jean-Louis was a strong and willing helper, he was no yachtsman and never really saw the point in a voyage for which he could see no scientific justification. There was also an incident when he ate the whole of a special cheese that Willy had been hoarding and was promptly seasick, which shocked the fastidious skipper.

Another irritation to de Roos was the presence of a Canadian yacht, the *J.E.Bernier II*, already one year out of Montreal, whose owner Reál Bouvier was the exact opposite of de Roos in character. The Canadian yacht suffered frequent breakdowns because it had not been properly engineered. Before discovering this, de Roos had agreed to sail in company but soon regretted it as he was constantly being asked to help with repairs to the *J.E.Bernier II*'s faulty engine and gearbox. Fortunately for de Roos, the Canadian yacht broke down with some finality at Resolute though afterwards Bouvier had the cheek to write an article saying de Roos would not have succeeded without his help!

The year 1977 turned out to be something of a freak. Initially the two yachts had great difficulty making their way

up the coast of Greenland to the open water at the top of
Baffin Bay but thereafter had a remarkably easy passage in
what turned out to be the best ice year since records began in
1900. This is not to lessen de Roos's achievement in any way
but he certainly was fortunate in never encountering really
severe ice conditions.

Young Jean-Louis really wanted to leave the boat at
Resolute but de Roos persuaded him to continue for the next
section, which everyone agrees is the hardest part of the
Northwest Passage. Having two men aboard was of great
assistance as it enabled them to push on 24 hours a day
whenever conditions permitted and by 23 August they
reached *Gjöa* Haven. Here the young Belgian finally parted
company with de Roos who had little alternative but to carry
on alone. This he did with great determination, driving
himself to exhaustion and beyond in his effort to make every
inch of progress while it was still possible. The long stretch
from the Mackenzie River along the north coast of Alaska was
the hardest as, with no shelter and strong winds he was forced
to keep going with virtually no chance to rest though at least
he managed to obtain some help from his autopilot from
Cambridge Bay onwards.

By the beginning of September, de Roos felt he was at the
limit of his endurance but although the weather continued to
be foul, with constant gales and sleet, the sea remained open
and *Williwaw* sailed on, finally reaching the relative safety of
the Bering Strait on the 18th. At last de Roos could heave-to
in safety and get some sleep! His achievement was extraordinary; not only was he the first yachtsman to sail through the
Northwest Passage but he had done it in one season and more
than a third of the distance had been single-handed. His book
on this voyage makes thrilling reading.

One has to accept that luck plays a large part in arctic
navigation. Sometimes the door is open and at others it is
firmly locked and bolted. To illustrate this one only needs to

contrast Willy de Roos's triumphant passage in 1977 with the efforts of American yachtsman John Bockstoce. His 18.9m (62ft) steel motor-sailer *Belvedere* was specially adapted for the Arctic, having a strong hull, powerful diesel engine, radar and every other modern device that money can buy, in spite of which it took him five years to get through.

Having spent one winter at Resolute, and a further two at Tuktoyaktuk, the troublesome *J.E. Bernier II* finally emerged in 1979 to become the second yacht (or third if you count *Gjöa*) to make successful transits of the passage. The next was the redoubtable Japanese yachtsman Keniche Horie who also took three years to get through in his sloop *Mermaid*. Horie made some of the stages alone and some with his wife and afterwards completed an epic circumnavigation of the American Continent.

In 1983 american John Bockstoce began his attempt to make the first west-east yacht passage in his ketch *Belvedere*. He was actually overtaken by another yacht *Vagabond II* which managed to reach Gjöa Haven before bedding down for two winters. Both these expeditions 'broke out' at the same time as me and we passed in opposite directions (see chapter 7). At the time, I had just been overtaken by Rick Thomas in his steel ketch *Northanger*, making 1988 by far the busiest season in arctic history, with four yachts in the Northwest Passage in addition to five ships.

Finally, there was the 5.5m (18ft) Hobiecat *Perception* on which two Canadians Jeff MacInnis and Mike Beedell pushed, pulled, paddled and sailed from Inuvik to Pond Inlet (off Lancaster Sound) during the summers of 1986 and 1988. As the Canadian arctic expert Tom Pullen pointed out in his review of their book, this was a full 1,100 miles short of being a transit of the Northwest Passage which is defined as being from Davis Strait to Bering Strait. To give them credit, MacInnis and Beedell do not claim to have made a proper transit of the passage, though plenty of others do on their behalf.

After Amundsen in 1906, there were no more attempts on the Northwest Passage until the Second World War but after that, the pace of development began to quicken. Construction of the Distant Early Warning Line of radar stations and later the discovery of oil in Alaska made it necessary to supply the Arctic and powerful icebreakers were built by both Canada and the United States as a result. According to Tom Pullen, my passage in *Mabel E.Holland* was transit No.46, while 19 of the previous ones had been by icebreakers.

When you look at the chart, the most obvious route is straight through Lancaster Sound, Parry Channel, M'Clure Strait and thence out into the Chukchi Sea but for the reasons we have already seen, no surface vessel has ever been able to do this. In 1960 however, a most significant passage was made by the nuclear-powered submarine *USS Sea Dragon* which glided silently through the deep-water channel under the ice. For this type of vessel, at least, the Northwest Passage is indeed a practical waterway and one which we are led to believe is now used regularly. In fact, a nuclear submarine wishing to travel from, say Russia to the Pacific does not even need to take the risk of entering the narrow straits of the Northwest Passage as she can steer due north, passing beneath the pole and surfacing in the Bering Strait. For them the 'open polar sea' is a reality.

Chapter 3

The seaman's apprenticeship

I HAVE often been asked how I came to be so involved with boats and although I believe there was an 18th Century book of sailing by someone named Cowper I have no idea if he was a relative and can't lay claim to any glorious seagoing achievements on the part of my forebears. My main influence in this direction was my father who was a keen sea angler and owned a series of motor boats.

This was his relaxation from business in Newcastle-upon-Tyne and I always looked forward to going with him on his summer fishing trips. His first boat was a 7.6m (25ft) clinker-built converted ship's lifeboat of the kind that was many people's introduction to boating in the early post-war years but they don't make terribly satisfactory launches and he soon changed to a conventional motor cruiser. Sadly, he then suffered a serious heart attack and had to sell this boat but in due course was well enough to buy a small launch with an aft cockpit for fishing. This in turn was replaced by a similar but larger boat while his final craft was a 9.1m (30ft) fishing boat by Tyrell of Arklow.

These boats were normally kept at Scarborough and in those days it was still possible to catch fish in the North Sea. He was not really interested in cruising for its own sake and his longest trip was usually to Filey and back but these outings were the high-spots of my summer holidays and I always dreamed of having a boat of my own.

During my years at Stowe School, I spent as much time as possible in the workshop where I built a 4.3m (14ft) dinghy. I longed to use the school sailing dinghies which cruised around so visibly on the ornamental lake beyond the games pitches but was not allowed to because I could not swim. For some unknown reason I used to suffer from feelings of panic when I got into a swimming pool and only managed to overcome this and learn to swim relatively recently. Before any smart psychologist rushes to the conclusion that I did all these trips to conquer my fear of water, I hasten to say that I always wanted to be on boats; it was the feeling of sinking beneath the water that I did not care for.

In my final year at Stowe, the school acquired four single-seat skiffs and I was able to learn rowing thanks to the fact that the teacher concerned took my word for it when I said I could swim. Of course the joke was that a racing skiff is just about the most tippy boat you can find; you can capsize one just by 'catching a crab'.

It was around this time that 'Blondie' Hasler made his famous half-a-crown wager with Francis Chichester for a single-handed race across the Atlantic. There were five contenders in that first race in 1960 and I wished I could join them – not a very practical dream for a 17 year-old. Having won the first OSTAR (Observer Single-handed Trans-Atlantic Race), Chichester then made his most famous voyage, single-handed around the world. Like so many others, I was inspired by his achievement which fuelled my desire to sail across the great oceans of the world.

Life's realities ensured that I could not fulfil this dream, for the time being, but after I had left school and gone to London to qualify as a Chartered Surveyor, I paid a visit to the Lymington office of the famous yacht designers Laurent Giles and Partners. They had designed the seaworthy Vertue Class and then the slightly larger Wanderer for the famous cruising couple Eric and Susan Hiscock. After long discussions with 'Jack' Giles I bought a set of plans for the Wanderer Class. Having inherited a little money, I decided to take the plunge and in 1967 I ordered one of these boats from the yard of Robert Lambies on the River Tyne.

Well-known for their ship's lifeboats and Trinity House tenders, Lambies were keen to enter the yacht market and had taken on Alec Culverwell who had been a foreman at one of Scotland's best-known yards, McGruers of Clynder. They were most enthusiastic about building my boat which was specified to be constructed in teak with a Mercedes diesel engine, aluminium mast and blue Terylene sails, the price being £5,500 all found. She was a splendid piece of work and was launched by the largest crane on the River Tyne, the North Eastern Marine crane at Parsons Marine and she was christened *Airedale*, not after the Yorkshire dog but Lord Cardigan's yacht aboard which he had lived in great style during the Crimean War.

Bursting with pride at owning my very own yacht and with the help of a friend Mike Gasper, I sailed her down to Scarborough. As I was working in London at the time, I soon realized it would be more practical to keep *Airedale* in East Anglia so that I could sail at the weekends and in 1969 moved her to Pin Mill on the Orwell and later to Woodbridge where I got a berth at Whisstocks Boatyard. By this time I was married and Woodbridge was my wife's home town so keeping the boat there was an ideal arrangement for us both.

When I proposed to Caroline she said she could not accept until she was sure she liked sailing. Fortunately she took to it and during the summer months we would cruise to Holland or down Channel to Brittany, steadily building up experience and confidence in the boat. On my weekday evenings in London, I would attend the King Edward VII Nautical College in East India Dock Road – still quite a seedy area at that time – to study for the old Board of Trade Yachtmaster Certificate which was terribly academic and impractical compared to today's RYA Yachtmaster test but taught me all about celestial navigation. One year, we managed to find time for a proper long cruise to Scotland and round the Hebridean Islands. In retrospect I was very lucky to own such a handsome, seaworthy cruising yacht while still in my late 20's and without too many responsibilities and it was altogether a very happy time.

In the back of my mind, I always had the idea of entering for either the single-handed transatlantic or the Round Britain Race. Both were organized by the Royal Western Yacht Club at Plymouth and alternated every two years. I did not feel qualified to tackle the Atlantic in 1972 so instead entered for the 1974 Round Britain Race. This was a two-handed event and I teamed up with a Scottish laird named Colin Lindsey McDougall. It was a pretty windy race but *Airedale* performed reasonably well, with no breakages and we were happy to finish 35th overall and 20th on handicap out of a fleet of 61 yachts.

With this experience under my belt, I felt sufficiently confident to enter the 1976 OSTAR. This turned out to be another heavy-weather race in which two lives were lost, one being the larger-than-life ex-Marine Colin McMullen who was sailing a bright yellow trimaran named *Three Cheers*. It was a most tragic story as just days before the start of the race his wife Bridget was electrocuted when she dropped an electric sander into the water while working on *Three Cheers*.

A number of yachts retired from the race with damage of various kinds but the strongly-built *Airedale* came through without a scratch and I felt very happy to finish 68th and 35th on handicap in the big fleet of 125, especially as she was one of the smaller boats competing.

Airedale was an excellent, sea-kindly cruising yacht but not particularly fast and I now wanted to move up to something more competitive so I took the decision to offer her for sale in the United States. Rather to my surprise the broker in Newport found a buyer remarkably quickly but after concluding the sale I felt quite guilty in parting with my first yacht which had proved such a good friend and looked after me well.

Needing a ride back to England, I teamed up with Jock McLeod who had also done the OSTAR in his very remarkable junk-rigged yacht *Ron Glas* which he boasted could be sailed in carpet slippers as she was totally enclosed, with all control lines led inside the wheelhouse. On the way we stopped at Halifax, Nova Scotia to pick up a Canadian called Bob Browne who had asked to do a passage in *Ron Glas* because he was considering fitting a junk rig to his own yacht. Unfortunately, Bob was seasick the whole way across the Atlantic, losing a lot of weight in the process. Whenever he was not feeling too dreadful I used to feed Bob with Complan, which I had often found was the only thing I could keep down when the going got rough and he came to believe I had saved his life by so doing.

As a result Bob became a stalwart friend and supporter who has helped and encouraged me with my various projects ever since. Perhaps the most important thing he did was introduce me to Captain Tom Pullen, Canada's foremost expert on arctic navigation, who really became my mentor for the Northwest Passage. I am always amazed how chance meetings of this kind can shape one's life.

For the time being, however, my ambition was to sail round the world and once back in England I again approached Laurent Giles for a suitable design. Unfortunately Jack Giles, one of the really great names of yacht design, had recently died but his colleague Dick Stower undertook to develop a design for me. This turned out to be a fairly conventional heavy-duty sloop of 12.8m (42ft) in length with a traditional long keel. The only unusual feature was that she was designed for aluminium construction which I felt had great merits and was still relatively new in those days.

The next step was to choose a builder experienced in aluminium construction and the one that stood out head and shoulders above the rest was Wolter Huisman of Vollenhove in Holland. I therefore signed a contract with them to build my new boat but soon ran into difficulties caused by the raging inflation that was going on at the time. When Harold Wilson devalued the pound, the price of my Dutch-built yacht suddenly leapt and I thought the only possibility would be to take delivery of her as a bare hull and have the fitting out done in England.

I went to Holland to discuss this with Huisman and noticed that alongside my boat was the hull of a 12.5m (41ft) Sparkman and Stephens design that the yard was planning to complete as a stock product. It had a very distinguished pedigree as not only were Sparkman and Stephens of New York the top designers of racing yachts, with innumerable America's Cup and Admiral's Cup winners to their credit, but this particular model was based on Edward Heath's *Morning Cloud IV*. It was obviously a much more race-oriented design than my Laurent Giles and I was most impressed by the strong construction and general air of purpose and efficiency. I therefore negotiated a swap, whereby Huisman took my Laurent Giles in exchange for a part-completed Huisman 41.

They delivered the new boat as a completed hull and deck with hatches, mast and deck gear, engine and stern gear but totally bare inside. With the help of three friends I motored her across the North Sea to Woodbridge where Whisstocks were to undertake the fitting out. This turned out to be an excellent arrangement as I could keep a close eye on progress, work on her myself at weekends and generally make sure everything was just as I wanted. Completed in June 1979 and christened *Ocean Bound*, she proved to be a real performer, especially to windward.

My intention was to sail around the world singlehanded and try to beat the record held by Sir Francis Chichester in *Gipsy Moth IV*. During that year, the state of Western Australia was celebrating its 150th anniversary and the Parmelia Race was organized from Plymouth to Perth with a stopover at Cape Town. This was for fully-crewed yachts, mostly larger than *Ocean Bound* so I thought it would be a good incentive to try to 'pace' this fleet for the first half of my circumnavigation. At one time, Caroline and I thought we could do the race together but the arrival of our son Freddie in July 1978 had made this impossible and Caroline gamely accepted the role of back-up crew, one she has often been called upon to fill since. In fact, she was mainly responsible for assembling and organizing the mountain of supplies needed to make me fully independent for a year.

As we were by now living in Newcastle, we made all the final preparations at Blyth and after a giving a party at the yacht club for numerous friends who had helped us, with *Ocean Bound* fully prepared and provisioned, we sailed down to Plymouth, arriving a week before the start of the Parmelia Race.

It was during our final week of preparation at Plymouth that the Fastnet Race was struck by a severe storm in the Western Approaches, resulting in the death of 15 people. Five yachts sank and 19 more were abandoned, the worst disaster in the history of offshore racing. The whole nation was shocked and it was extremely sobering to think that I was willingly putting myself at this kind of risk. In fact, it turned out that the Fastnet fleet had met once-in-a-lifetime conditions in which a sudden change of wind direction caused exceptionally big, unstable waves. The subsequent inquiry by the Royal Ocean Racing Club also pointed to numerous deficiencies in the boats, such as hatch boards that could fall out if the yacht inverted and batteries that were not securely held down. Liferafts, which most yachtsmen assumed to be the ultimate refuge, turned out to be dangerously inadequate in some cases.

In a somewhat sombre mood therefore, I said goodbye to Caroline and Freddie. No insurance company was prepared to take on the risk of *Ocean Bound* but I had taken out two life policies so that my family would not actually starve if the ocean swallowed me up. Of course all the gloom was forgotten as soon as I got under way and during a very respectable passage to Cape Town, keeping up well with the Parmelia yachts, the worst thing that happened was one knock-down during which I received a painful rope-burn letting off the sheets in a hurry. The incredible ability of rumour to travel and multiply was amply demonstrated after I recounted this relatively minor matter by radio to one of the Parmelia competitors, *Bounty*. An Australian journalist on board her sent a story to his paper, improving it a bit in the telling, and it eventually got back to Caroline in Newcastle that *Ocean Bound* had 'capsized' and that I had been 'badly burned'. Naturally, she was frantic with worry until she heard via another yacht that the rope burn was nearly better and that *Ocean Bound* had suffered no damage whatever!

Long range radio communication from small boats was not nearly as good then as it is now and I had a ludicrous time trying to send a message to Caroline asking her to assemble various bits of gear and bring them to Cape Town. I passed this message by radio to Peter Morris on board *Mabena* who very kindly telephoned Caroline using their powerful single sideband set but when she tried to respond a few days later with the information that everything was organized, my own set had packed up. Finally, I crossed tracks with an Italian yacht, *Golden Lion* and we sailed along shouting at each other through loud-hailers. They then called up *Mabena* so that her crew would not think I was in trouble. There are times when I agree with Blondie Hasler that it would be better to drown like a gentleman than entrust your life to a radio set.

Anyway, I reached Cape Town after a respectable 57 days to be met by Caroline who had been staying with friends. I stayed for a week during which I put right various minor problems and then sailed again with the intention of continuing non-stop as far as Wellington, New Zealand. Unfortunately this did not quite work out as when I was approaching Bass Strait (between Australia and Tasmania) in very heavy weather, the Sailomat self-steering system was wrenched off the transom, breaking all the brackets in the process. Fortunately it was held by a safety lanyard or the whole lot would have gone to the bottom. I was carrying an Aries self-steerer as a back-up and with a great deal of difficulty in the heavy seas managed to fit it onto the stern. However as I was then quite close to Cape Otway, I decided to put into Apollo Bay, only 15 miles north-east of the cape, to sort things out, especially as there was also a problem with the engine and I had hurt my knee from constant kneeling on the non-slip deck and wanted to find some medical attention.

During this section of the trip I had enjoyed much better radio contact using the 'ham' network of radio amateurs. Most ham operators are dedicated enthusiasts who are only too pleased to help and I was able to speak regularly to a South African who very kindly passed on messages to our local newspaper in Newcastle and to Caroline. Thanks to him, I knew that she and Freddie were now in Australia, staying with my cousin. I gave her a terrific shock by telephoning her at Christopher's house but urged her not to rush down to Apollo Bay as I wanted to set off again as soon a possible.

In this I was greatly helped by Don McIntyre and his girlfriend Debbie who were working on their yacht *Skye* in which they planned to sail round Australia. More recently, Don has competed in the 1991/2 BOC Challenge single-handed round the World race. He and Debbie were an absolute tower of strength and have remained good friends ever since. Two local fishermen Ross and Harry Ferrier also pitched in and gave a lot of practical assistance fitting up the Aries steering gear. To my amazement, Don and Debbie offered to travel to New Zealand to help me fit new rigging, which I had decided to do at the half-way point.

In what seemed no time, I was ready to set off again and was thoroughly glad that everything was in proper order as I was hit by very severe weather in the Bass Strait with winds gusting to 80 knots. But everything held together and I had a fairly uneventful passage across the Tasman before receiving another dose of heavy weather approaching Wellington. It was so windy I had to take refuge in a small bay on D'Urville Island during which time Wellington Airport was closed when the wind reached 100 knots! Meanwhile Caroline had been invited to go up in a helicopter with a TV crew to look for me and was thoroughly alarmed by the conditions and was ordered to return to Wellington to wait for the weather to improve. When it had calmed down a bit I sailed into 'Windy Wellington' to be greeted by Caroline, Freddie and Caroline's sister Diana who had come over for the Christmas holidays, plus Don and Debbie. I reached Evans Bay Marina just before midnight on New Year's Eve so naturally we had a big celebration.

We had been lent a house in Wellington and had a wonderfully social time for a few days. In spite of very cold weather, Don fitted a complete set of new rigging and serviced the winches. We gave *Ocean Bound* a complete check after sailing half-way round the World but there was remarkably little to be done other than routine cleaning and re-stowing. After a week I was ready to set off again, receiving a tremendous send-off from the boat-mad Kiwis. The only slight problem was that I had forgotten to file one particular Customs and Immigration form and while passing Chatham Island received a radio message asking me to return to Wellington to regularize the matter. Fortunately Caroline was able to straighten matters out with the British Consul and humbly apologize on my behalf.

The long passage across the Southern Ocean was uneventful and my first experience of Cape Horn a positive anticlimax as it was sunny and almost calm as I sailed sedately past at a distance of about five miles. I then 'turned left' into the South Atlantic, passing the Falkland Islands and making a short stopover at Rio de Janeiro. There I collected a parcel of supplies including a light genoa generously paid for by Tyne Tees TV and some special batteries for my Plessey radio. Caroline had the luck to have these sent out in the diplomatic bag, after delivering them personally to No.10 Downing Street!

Wrenching myself away from the flesh-pots of Rio it was on into the tropics, across the Equator and the trade-winds belt, making excellent progress until I reached Cape Finisterre where the chilly blast of a typical April northeasterly did its very best to stop me reaching home. After an uncomfortable beat across the Bay of Biscay, I finally reached Plymouth on St George's Day, 23rd April 1980 to a most heart-warming welcome including lots of flattering attention from the Press. I had been away for 247 days of which 224 had been spent at sea – just two days less than Sir Francis Chichester's time. This was a new record for a singlehanded circumnavigation of the world and earned me a place in the Guinness Book of Records.

During the next few days I received more than 500 telegrams while TV and radio stations all over the world carried reports of my voyage. I was quite overwhelmed by the attention after so long alone. After catching my breath for a couple of days at Plymouth, I sailed *Ocean Bound* on to receive three civic welcomes: at Woodbridge, at my native city of Newcastle and also at Blyth.

Many of the people I spoke to after my return seemed genuinely surprised that I should have enjoyed the voyage, thinking I would have been lonely, bored or daunted by the hardships. I was able to tell them with complete honesty that I was ready to do it all again and after saying this a few hundred times I added, facetiously at first, that my next project would be to 'unwind' by sailing round the world in the opposite direction.

The only person to have done this was Chay Blyth in his 1970-71 singlehanded circumnavigation in the 18m (59ft) ketch *British Steel*, the so-called 'impossible voyage' against the prevailing winds. I was convinced it was anything but impossible and finally reached a decision to have a crack at bettering Chay's time of 292 days.

During the next winter I slowly made my preparations and in May 1981 sailed *Ocean Bound* over to Holland so that Huisman's could re-fair the underwater profile to produce a really smooth bottom. On such a long voyage, a speed increase of 10 percent would reduce the time taken by the enormous margin of 20 days so any improvement would be well worthwhile. To cope with the heavy pounding to windward, a new heavier-section mast was fitted together with new rigging. I also added two new sails to the existing wardrobe. Then it was back to the Tyne for tuning up and provisioning ready for the now-familiar passage to Plymouth.

This time I delayed my departure until 22 September which I calculated would allow me to sail me down to Cape Horn in the early part of the summer in the Southern Hemisphere, so as to make use of the best of the weather and daylight during the long, long haul round the globe and back to the Atlantic. Instead of making a stop at Rio, which is some way off the shortest course to Cape Horn, I sailed straight to the Falkland Islands, arriving at Stanley Harbour on the 15th November 1981 in the teeth of a 45-knot gale. After a three-day stop during which I thoroughly checked the whole boat to make her ready for the ordeal to come, I was off towards the notorious Cape Horn.

There are two reasons that Cape Horn has such a fearsome reputation. The first is that Drake Strait, between the southern tip of Tierra del Fuego and Graham Land, which projects north from the Antarctic Continent is relatively narrow at approximately 500 miles so that every depression that comes rumbling across the Southern Ocean eventually has to squeeze through this gap and there is no way for a vessel negotiating Cape Horn to avoid the resulting gales. Secondly, the depth of water decreases sharply as you come onto the continental shelf and this causes the big ocean swells to break, causing very dangerous steep seas.

After my exceptionally mild introduction to Cape Horn the previous year it was clear that I had had my ration of easy times. This time my arrival coincided with a series of gales that just seemed to keep coming one after the other. Every time I thought I had got past the dreaded cape, I was hurled back again, only breaking through into the Pacific after ten days of thoroughly unpleasant sailing. The cold, the wet, the violent motion and the incessant high-pitched shriek of the wind is incredibly wearing and saps one's strength and morale in an insidious way.

Reading over my log for that period I note that on the 21st November I naively wrote:

"Hopefully round The Horn tomorrow."

Four days later it was a very different story:

"Survived the night, through gigantic seas and tremendous wind especially in the gusts which could easily have been at 100 miles an hour. The water becomes white-over as day is turned into darkness as very dark clouds descend over the area. This lasts for about half an hour and then the wind drops to its usual 50 knots. Sometimes there is respite in the deep valleys as one then becomes protected from the wind only to rise again to its mighty blast. It is very cold as there are frequent hail showers. The boat occasionally is engulfed in a foam bath of spray and spume and I don't know how she survives it.....the deck is a turmoil of sails and sheets lashed down as it became too dangerous to take them off."

By the 28th November I had just about reached the end of my tether. I had still not managed to get past the Horn and conditions down below were becoming increasingly chaotic and unpleasant. At that most dismal hour of the day, 0100, I scrawled in the logbook:

"Once again storm force winds, I must seriously now consider giving up. I am very tired my judgement is becoming impaired."

But in the nick of time, on the very same day, conditions began to improve. The wind and sea moderated to Force 6 and I was able to set the mainsail once more and make progress to the west. Before the end of the day I was tacking up the Chilean coastline and admiring the snow-covered mountains glittering in the sunshine.

Once 'off soundings' as the old sailors used to say, the seas became more regular and I settled down to the endless beat to windward, keeping more or less between the 45th and 50th parallels of latitude. There's not really too much one can say about this passage except that it just goes on and on and on in a steady routine of eating, sleeping, navigating and changing sail area as the wind increased or decreased. Chay Blyth had suffered the misfortune of losing his self-steering during this part of the voyage with the result that *British Steel* only made good progress to windward while he was steering by hand. Thankfully, my Aries worked perfectly and provided one set everything up carefully would sail *Ocean Bound* to windward almost as well as I could. And of course she does sail well to windward and in my opinion is just about the ideal size for one person to control.

Around Christmas time I exchanged greetings on the radio with another singlehander Paul Rogers who passed in the opposite direction when we were at a longitude of 140° West. Most of New Year's Day was spent becalmed – a pretty unusual experience in this part of the world! Since there is little risk of meeting another vessel in this totally desolate region, I could let the Aries get on with the job and enjoy a reasonable amount of sleep whenever there was no urgent work to be done. As a result I did not suffer the extreme exhaustion, hallucinations and so on that made Chay's voyage so incredibly gruelling. I was also making considerably faster progress.

South of New Zealand I had some anxious times passing Stewart Island where there are some isolated outcrops of rocks called The Snares and The Traps. As on my first circumnavigation, I was totally dependant on sextant sights for position fixing and when it is cloudy one just had to keep up the dead reckoning as accurately as possible but on this occasion I had a bit of luck when I fell in with a Japanese fish factory ship. We talked on the VHF radio and they confirmed my position to three places of decimals!

After New Zealand the next objective was Tasmania and conditions in the Tasman Sea were severe but I was greatly cheered by making radio contact with Ross Ferrier, the fisherman from Apollo Bay who had been so helpful on my previous trip. I had always planned to stop at Albany, close to the south-west 'corner' of Australia, where Caroline and Freddie were waiting. Another reason for wanting to go ashore was an recurrence of the knee problem that had troubled me before. When the weather was bad, most of the jobs on deck had to be done kneeling and the rough non-skid surface brought on a painful swelling that made working very uncomfortable.

I eventually arrived at Albany on 10th February, 83 days out of Port Stanley. Of that time, only three days had not been spent sailing to windward. It truly was 'the wrong way round.' People at Albany were amazed to see goose-barnacles growing along the topsides of *Ocean Bound* and verdigris along the toe rail because she had been heeled the same way for weeks on end.

In addition to Caroline and Freddie, my mother who had recently remarried after twenty years of widowhood had come over for a holiday with her new husband and my invaluable friend Don McIntyre turned up as ready to help as ever. Nick Franklin who designed the Aries self-steering gear came to see how his latest model was behaving and I was delighted to tell him that it had worked perfectly the whole way.

During the next few days the whole boat was checked and serviced from stem to stern and all the stores checked and re-stowed. The bottom was cleaned off and the barnacles scraped away so that *Ocean Bound* looked as good as new again. We even had time to relax and do a little sight-seeing for a couple of days.

After leaving Albany I took a gamble by going up to 32° South which involved sailing further but was rewarded by strong beam winds which enabled me to reach Cape Town in the very fast time of only 35 days. As I approached South Africa I was able to make radio contact again with Paul Rogers. Unfortunately he was having problems with his boat *Spirit of Pentax* and had to put into Cape Town for repairs. I thought that perhaps he would give me a race back to England but his repairs took too long and I hurried on after only four days in harbour.

The final stage from Cape Town back to England was again relatively fast, taking only 47 days. The main frustration was being becalmed for 48 hours in the Western Approaches but at least I did not have to buck the wretched north-easterlies across the Bay of Biscay this time. After leaving Cape Town I heard on the radio that the Falklands had been invaded by Argentina and that a British force was on its way to the South Atlantic to expel them. Envisaging a vast armada of ships ploughing their way towards the Falklands I became quite worried and kept an extra-vigilant watch but in fact never saw a single warship or aircraft!

On the 17th of May 1982 I sailed back into Plymouth to a second warm welcome but this time I was far from being the main attraction as the Sound was a scene of great activity as the fleet of ferries and cargo vessels prepared to sail for the Falklands. At the same time the Pope was making his first visit to England and Prince William was born! Nevertheless I was extremely satisfied to have sliced 72 days off Chay Blyth's time for the voyage. I was now the only person to have sailed singlehanded round the world in both directions and also held the record for the fastest single-handed time in each direction, earning another entry in the Guinness Book of Records. The really interesting thing was that the total trip was ten days shorter and the time spent at sea had been three days less than when I had sailed round the world in the conventional direction, so I could genuinely claim that 'It was quicker backwards!'

Chapter 4

First sail, now power

On my visits to Woodbridge I noticed that two 12.8m (42ft) Watson lifeboats were stored at Whisstocks Boatyard awaiting a decision on their future. I passed them regularly, never failing to be impressed by their immensely sturdy, seaworthy appearance and presently heard on the grapevine that one of these boats would shortly be coming up for sale, which gave me the germ of an idea. Having by now sailed singlehandedly around the world in each direction, I was looking for a fresh challenge and it occurred to me that I might have a shot at becoming the first person to *motor* around the world alone. However when I mentioned this idea to members of my immediate family, it was clear that they thought it was a completely hare-brained idea and it was obvious that I was not going to receive much support from that quarter.

Initially, I did no more than ask the RNLI to put me on their mailing list for news of forthcoming sales but this bore fruit quite quickly when tender documents for one of the boats lying at Woodbridge arrived in January 1983, giving me until March to decide whether to make a bid. During that time I commissioned a designer to work out whether the fuel capacity could be increased sufficiently to give a range of at least 5,000 nautical miles and his calculations indicated that this could be achieved within the limits of stability. I therefore sent in a bid of a little over £10,000 and shortly afterwards became the owner of the 12.8m (42ft) Watson beach type lifeboat *Mabel E.Holland*.

.If this seems remarkably little money for a boat that would cost in the region of £250,000 to build today, it must be understood that due to their layout and construction, RNLI lifeboats do not make good motor cruisers. For their size, there is extraordinarily little accommodation space. Any glass-fibre motor cruiser half the size has a larger cabin. They are also quite difficult to handle and need specialized maintenance. In fact a lifeboat makes a pretty impractical vessel for private ownership and this accounts for the relatively low prices they fetch.

Mabel E.Holland was built in 1956 at the yard of the best-known of the RNLI's contractors William Osborne of Littlehampton and she was a 12.8m (42ft) beach-type lifeboat designed by the Scottish naval architects G.L.Watson. The difference between these boats and other lifeboats lies in the way they were launched.

There are a number of lifeboat stations, such as Dungeness, where there is no harbour and a loose shingle beach making it impossible to have a permanent slipway into the sea. In these cases the RNLI usually constructs a short slipway above high-water mark which is supplemented by a pathway of greased timbers which are laid out just prior to launching. On being released, the lifeboat gathers speed down the slipway and if all goes well slithers over the timbers and into the sea. Sometimes the boat fails to break through the surf and then takes an awful pounding until she either manages to break clear or is dragged out of the water. This happened to *Mabel E. Holland* at least once during her service at Dungeness.

The system for recovering the boats at such stations is also fairly dramatic. They just run in until they hit the beach whereupon a shore party dashes into the surf to connect a wire to a strop running through an aperture in the keel after which a powerful winch drags the boat up the beach. It does not take much imagination to see that no normally designed and constructed boat would survive such treatment for very long.

Beach lifeboats are therefore beamy, shallow and fairly flat-bottomed so that they can sit on the ground without falling over and are tremendously strongly built. They are good load-carriers which was vital for my purpose and designed to operate in shallow water. Because of the need to survive hitting the bottom without being disabled, the twin propellers turn inside what are called 'tunnels.' These are actually semi-circular recesses in the underside of the hull which enable the props to go on turning even when the boat is hard aground. The rudder can slide up and down a metal shaft and was only dropped after the boat had got clear of the beach.

Conceived in the late 1940s when ships still had completely open lifeboats, *Mabel E. Holland* was little different, originally having just a windscreen to shield the cox'n as he stood on a platform behind the wheel, with his legs astride the steering shaft. At a later date the windscreen was extended to give wrap-around sides and a small roof but this shelter was still completely open on its aft face. It was only after I bought her that she acquired a full wheelhouse with a watertight door.

Her design stability allowed her to carry up to 70 survivors, in theory, though heaven knows where they would have been fitted in. Even with the small 'survivor's cabin' jammed full, it would have been necessary for the others to sit shoulder to shoulder right round the decks and as these become awash in heavy weather, conditions would have been abominable. Shelter did not receive a high priority in those days.

There was considerable controversy at the time about whether lifeboats should be made self-righting or merely very stable. This was well before horrors such as the Longhope and Penlee lifeboat disasters convinced the RNLI that all their boats should be self-righting. At the time *Mabel E.Holland* was built, it was felt that self-righters had a jerky motion and therefore gave their crew a more uncomfortable time. Watson believed it was better to have a wide, low hull that would be very hard to upset. The low decks shed water immediately and even the crew cockpit was self-draining so that stability would not be affected if this area were flooded.

The construction was typical of lifeboats of the era being mainly timber. Framed in Canadian Rock Elm with oak keel, stem and stern-post, there were two layers of mahogany planking set at an angle to each other (the so-called 'double diagonal' method) with canvas soaked in grease and putty between the layers to improve the water-tightness. Four water-tight bulkheads divided the hull into six compartments and all spare space was taken up by cedar-wood 'air-cases' covered in painted canvas. Even if the hull was pierced, these air cases provided easily enough buoyancy to keep the vessel afloat. In fact there were instances of the crew failing to notice that a lifeboat had been holed because there was so little difference in the performance.

As a lifeboat, her accommodation began with a small radio and survivors' cabin right forward, accessible via a deck hatch. This was a veritable 'black hole of Calcutta' as, with the hatch shut, there was no view from within and no natural lighting. Communication with the rest of the crew was by voice pipe. I can only suppose that RNLI radio operators had very strong stomachs.

The engine-room was just forward of amidships, occupying the broadest part of the hull and this is the main reason that lifeboats make poor motor-cruisers. This vital compartment had water-tight bulkheads at each end and a double bottom, making it as nearly impregnable as could be. In it were mounted the two Gardner 4LW naturally-aspirated diesel engines, rated at 48 shaft horsepower each. By modern standards this is a very modest power output but it is important to realize that high speed is not possible with this kind of heavy-displacement hull and that ability to tow was more important. Turning 26in propellers via a 2:1 reduction gearbox, these engines produced considerable 'bollard pull' and were exceptionally reliable and economical.

One of the requirements was that the engines must be capable of being started up and put into gear with the boat still on dry land so that the boat ran down the slipway with the screws already turning. To this end the exhausts are of the dry type and the engine cooling was via a heat exchanger which in turn was cooled by seawater. This was important as it meant that salt water never ran through the engines themselves. The prop shafts ran through sealed tubes filled with a special oil so that the bearings would not seize through running dry.

When built in 1956, *Mabel* could boast full electric lighting, the power for this being generated by a Lucas 12-volt dynamo fitted to each engine. Amazingly, these dynamos gave me unfailing service through two circumnavigations and every possible extreme of climate, in spite of being 30 years old at the outset. The starboard engine also had a power take-off which drove a capstan on deck.

The engine-room door opens into a small covered area with benches on either side where the crew of eight men would sit and this became my main cabin. The steering wheel is mounted centrally at the aft end of this. The tradition of the Royal National Lifeboat Institution is to name their boats according to the wishes of generous benefactors. When

Mabel Holland died, her sister Maud made a large donation to the RNLI in her memory, which resulted in lifeboat O.N. 937 being named *Mabel E.Holland.*

She served for 22 years as the Dungeness Lifeboat during which time she was launched on service no fewer than 198 times and rescued 67 people. Perhaps her most noteworthy service was on 2nd February 1974 when she was launched in hurricane force winds to take an injured seaman off the tanker *Merc Texaco.* In enormous seas it took many attempts to transfer the injured man and the cox'n Bert Tart was awarded the RNLI's Silver Medal in recognition of his superb seamanship on this service. After retiring from the Dungeness position, *Mabel* served a further four years in the reserve fleet. Her most important station during this period was Aldeburgh in Suffolk which has a shingle beach rather similar to Dungeness. When Aldeburgh received a new Rother Class lifeboat, *Mabel* was laid up at nearby Woodbridge where I first came across her.

I was delighted to make the purchase so easily and proud to own a boat with such a distinguished record although, as I say, there was a distinct coolness from the family over this purchase. Before launching her at Woodbridge I had the hull sand-blasted and re-painted, damaged deck-covering removed and all the 'air-cases' taken out. She was then launched and I was almost immediately asked if I would provide an escort across the North Sea for a lady who suffered from an unusual kidney disease who wanted to gain publicity and raise money for fellow-sufferers by sailing to Ostend in a 3.6m (12ft) Firefly dinghy. This went well and created a certain amount of interest so I persuaded my secretary Beryl Turner to begin writing letters to potential sponsors to see if I could gain some support for my idea of a singlehanded motor circumnavigation.

Naively, I thought oil companies would jump at the idea of supporting a 'first' of this kind but their jumps turned out to be imperceptible! I had spoken to a public relations man in Newcastle named Geoff O'Connell who was working for a boat-building company called Bellway and was confident he could find sponsorship. During July I therefore motored the boat up to Newcastle, giving me a first experience of handling her on my own, and O'Connell laid on a press release and viewing day. The Newcastle Journal, which has always shown a keen interest in my expeditions, published a story but it was not followed up by any rush of gentlemen waving cheque-books. The whole idea was beginning to look like a washout so I took the boat down river to Albert Edward Dock at North Shields where I could leave her safely.

By sheer chance, because they were close to the dock, I called in at Smiths Ship-repairers, whose normal work was repairing Royal Fleet Auxiliaries and other commercial ships, to ask them how much they would charge to lift the lifeboat out and do various jobs on her. I met the Managing Director Ernie Ware who had seen the piece in the Newcastle Journal and in turn had spoken to his Chairman Denis Vernon about it. The shipping industry being in the doldrums, they had spare capacity at their yard and felt that it might raise morale and give them some useful publicity if they were to undertake the conversion work on *Mabel* as a form of sponsorship.

This fantastic offer was just what was needed to lift the project off the ground and I immediately drew up a specification of the work to done. Smiths reckoned it would take about three weeks to complete. About this time I heard that a Dutchman named Eilco Kasemier was also aiming to be the first to make a solo round-the-world voyage in a motor vessel and had obtained a specially designed and built vessel to do it in. He was apparently planning to set out at the end of September, so as far as I was concerned, the race was on, though time was extremely short.

In the second week of August, *Mabel* was lifted out of the water at Smiths and completely stripped out except for the

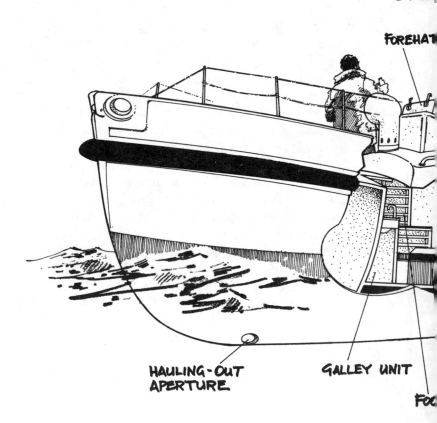

ENGINE
EXHA

FOREHAT

HAULING-OUT
APERTURE

GALLEY UNIT

FOO

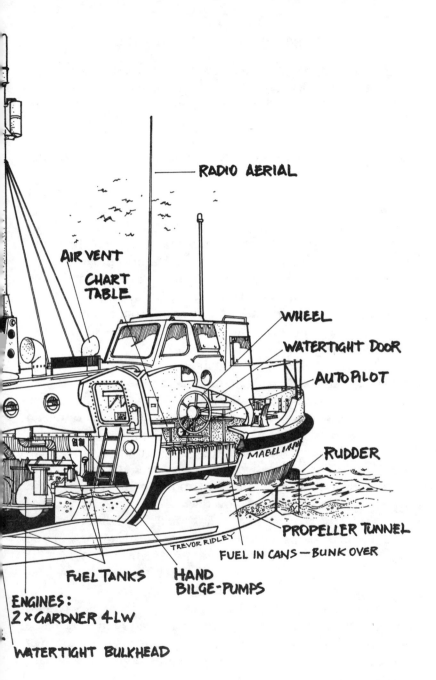

RADIO AERIAL

AIR VENT

CHART TABLE

WHEEL

WATERTIGHT DOOR

AUTOPILOT

RUDDER

MABEL MANN

TREVOR RIDLEY

PROPELLER TUNNEL

FUEL IN CANS — BUNK OVER

FUEL TANKS

HAND BILGE-PUMPS

ENGINES: 2 × GARDNER 4LW

WATERTIGHT BULKHEAD

engine-room. The shafts were drawn, and new seals and props fitted. Gardners had already agreed to service the engines and I had been to a maintenance course at their factory in Manchester.

The forward compartment was converted into a galley and food store, with a cooker and sink facing forward and rows of shelves on both sides. Four big heavy-duty batteries were fitted here so Smiths made a steel cover over them that formed a bench seat. As there is no standing headroom, one has to remain seated at all times when in the galley. This compartment was still only accessible via a hatch in the foredeck as it was not possible to break through the watertight bulkhead into the engine-room. As I obviously needed some kind of cabin in which to sleep and navigate, we decided that additional aluminium would be welded onto the existing steering shelter to turn it into a totally enclosed wheelhouse with a watertight door at the rear end.

The area which had contained the crew's benches became the cabin with a single bunk along the port side and a navigation table opposite. Between the two, another bench seat was constructed which doubled up as a 'loo, operating on the 'bucket and chuck it' principle. The simplest things work best. Again, headroom was limited, being no more than 1.37m (4ft 6in). Access to this compartment was distinctly restricted as there was only just room to squeeze past the wheel which could not be moved without major engineering.

In fact the steering system was a real pain. The cox'n used to stand on a grating with his legs on either side of the steering shaft and as I was not intending to remain on my feet for approximately 25,000 sea-miles, we built a saddle-seat over the shaft with foot-rests on either side. To steer standing up, one needed to be in front of the wheel with hands behind one's back! Just how the lifeboat cox'n had managed to see where he was going was not obvious as the visibility through the small and yellowing panes of armoured glass was appalling. This we were able to improve a bit by changing the armoured glass.

Even with the new enclosed wheelhouse, the interior was extremely cramped and nothing at all like the spacious cabin of *Ocean Bound*. People who came to see the boat seemed to suddenly develop a shaking motion of the head and obviously considered me quite mad.

As is usually the case, the refit took much longer than expected; not through any fault of the ever-helpful staff at Smiths but because so many suppliers were late or delivered wrongly-made items. For instance a firm on the South Coast were making a series of flexible fuel cells, carefully designed to fit into certain spaces, and calculated to hold 75 gallons each. When the first one arrived, it only held 30 gallons and the whole job had to be started again. As August turned to September I was working alongside the Smiths men every day and continuing late into the evenings after they had gone home. Friends came and joined me for weekend shifts, but by the third week of the month, when a whole host of equipment had still not arrived, it was obvious that I would not be able to leave that year and it was pointless to go on rushing things. I reconciled myself to the fact that Kasemier would almost certainly complete his motor circumnavigation before me and continued work under less pressure.

In the first week of November the boat was eventually ready for launching, looking extremely smart in her high-visibility livery of bright yellow hull and orange superstructure with red rubbing strake.

I spent the next few weeks on trials, taking the boat as far as Lymington and then back to Woodbridge to see what teething problems arose. The worst difficulty was in transferring fuel from the various temporary storage tanks and cans to the main wing tanks that supply the engines. The fillers for these were on the decks amidships and as the decks were frequently awash with seawater it was hard to stop it trickling into the fuel tanks. This was a problem I never really solved and keeping the tanks topped up at sea was always hard work. Another difficulty was with the outboard seals on the prop shafts which tended to admit seawater, causing the oil to emulsify.

During this period I was fortunate in obtaining another sponsor, Finnigans Paints who gave me £10,000 towards the project. This came about through the good offices of John Foster who admired my previous circumnavigations and had recently sold his company to the Hunting Group.

During the winter I kept the boat at Woodbridge and continued checking the equipment and gradually working her up to full efficiency. At the same time I was accumulating the usual mountain of stores, sufficient to keep me going for eight months. In March, after the boat had been back to Smith's for some further remedial work, I stowed everything on board and loaded the boat with 1,000 gallons of diesel fuel after which I set off for Plymouth. On arrival there, I met Eilco Kasemier who had just completed a very successful circum-navigation in his specially-built motorboat *Bylgia*. However I was secretly delighted to discover that he had been accom-panied by a friend for most of the time so that the first solo motor circumnavigation was still beckoning. We each looked over the other's boat: I with envy at the comfort and many labour-saving devices on *Bylgia* and he with disbelief at *Mabel E.Holland*. He told me later he was convinced I would never make it; not only because she was so uncomfortable but because the whole boat was so inconveniently laid out for single-handed operation.

Be that as it may, I departed from Plymouth on 16th April 1984 to the farewell waves of family, friends and well-wishers, bound for Horta in the Azores. This first long passage in the lifeboat turned out to be a reasonably unevent-ful and any doubts about how the boat would handle in bad weather were dispelled when we went through a severe gale.

The biggest problem was transferring fuel from cans into the main tanks when the decks were being continually washed by seas.

At Horta I refuelled for the next long leg to the Panama Canal and left on 28 April, running slap into another heavy gale, right on the nose. With the boat fully laden, she was very wet and I had to remain more or less permanently 'indoors' which is an odd feeling if you are used to a sailing yacht where you spend the majority of the time in the cockpit. Travelling through the Sargasso Sea I was continually bothered by weed becoming entangled in the propellers. After a quantity had built up, it would make an irritating noise as it slapped against the hull and I would then have to stop and clear it away.

Just before clearing the Sargasso Sea, I noticed that the Neox oil in the starboard propeller shaft was starting to go white and emulsify – a sure sign that it was contaminated with sea-water. Not having experienced this before I was worried that the bearing would not be receiving proper lubrication and decided to make a stop at Tortola in the British Virgin Islands rather than go straight on to the Panama Canal.

At Road Town, Tortola, the boat was slipped by Tortola Yachts whose engineer suggested an American gadget called a Speedi Sleeve made by American Rawhide. These proved very satisfactory but caused a delay as I had to wait for them to be ordered from the 'states. Meanwhile I was lucky enough to meet up with a man who had been an officer on a Polaris nuclear submarine and turned out to be a genius with electrical equipment. He gave my Lucas dynamos, which must have seemed very antiquated to him, a complete strip down and rebuild after which they worked faultlessly for two circumnavigations! Even better, he had recently begun working for Pusser's Rum and after consulting his boss presented me with a case of this fortifying beverage.

When this work was complete I set off for the Panama Canal but had another scare on the way when the fuel-injection pump on the starboard engine seized solid. This was most unusual on a Gardner engine and turned out to be due to a biocide which I had been advised to add to the fuel to prevent algal growth in the tanks; something that can be a serious problem in hot climates. Maybe I put in too much because it did the pump no good at all and I limped to Cristobal on one engine which I fed carefully on a diet of uncontaminated fuel.

At Cristobal I contacted a firm that was supposed to be the authorized CAV/Lucas agent and their engineer came and dismantled the pump and took it away. When I finally managed to get it back, it was in pieces with half the components missing, which I gathered was fairly typical of the 'service' one can expect in this part of the world. Fortunately I had also spoken to my secretary Beryl Turner who had arranged for Gardners to send out two new pumps and these were waiting at the airport together with a radio to replace a faulty one. The fun started when I tried to obtain customs clearance for these items. If you are not prepared to grease a lot of palms the game is to keep you shuttling endlessly between offices, which are all miles apart and usually shut.

Very fortunately my MP Neville Trotter, who had recently been to Panama, gave me a letter of introduction to the British High Commissioner who generously lent me a car and driver plus an official-looking letter of authorization. Thus armed, I got hold of my parcels within the hour! I had another stroke of luck when it turned out that a New Zealand yacht which was also waiting to go through the canal had the identical type of Gardner 4LW engine which the owner had totally rebuilt. So with me holding the works manual and him the spanners, we fitted the new pumps without recourse to any more local cowboys.

To pass through the canal, the boat must first be measured and registered for dues after which you are given a date and time of departure. You then have to book a pilot and you must also have four line-handlers on board. This job is no joke as the warps have to be over 30m (100ft) long each and strong enough to hold the boat against violent turbulence in the locks. Luckily, I was able to 'borrow' four people from a yacht with a crew of eight! Moreover, they arrived promptly at 4am which was the time we had been given for departure. We followed a huge Ro-Ro ship about 145m (800ft) long and 30m (100ft) wide. Entering the locks was not easy with so much turbulence in the water and on one occasion the lifeboat spun round in a complete circle.

There are three locks on the Atlantic side and three more at the Pacific end, with Gatun Lake and the impressive Culebra Cut in the middle. It rained continuously all day until we arrived at Balboa Yacht Club at about 4pm. I spent three days here stocking up with fuel and supplies as I planned to motor directly to Tahiti, a distance of about 5000 miles and just about the maximum possible range for *Mabel E.Holland*. I left without regrets on 13 June as the overall impression one receives of Panama is of hatred, fear and corruption.

On the way to Tahiti, I paid a short visit to Galapagos but visiting any of the wildlife reserves was impossible as they are heavily restricted and you have to apply for permission a long time ahead. A full month after leaving Panama, I reached Pepeete in Tahiti, arriving in the middle of a crowd of colourful canoes preparing for the regatta. The harbour was packed and I could just manage to squeeze between two motor yachts, much to their annoyance. While there I met Lorenzo and Mirella Riciardi who spotted me arriving and came over to look at the boat. Lorenzo had an Arab Dhow built for himself, using traditional methods and wrote a fascinating book about it illustrated by Mirella who is an outstanding photographer. Her grandfather was Philippe

77

Bunau-Varilla who was one of the driving forces behind the building of the Panama Canal and she was intrigued to see that I had bought a book about its history.

The next stage was to Fiji which proved fairly uneventful except for the final approaches which are barred by a complex series of reefs to the East of the island. These are very difficult to spot if there is any sea running and as I arrived in the dark I deemed it prudent to stop the engines and lie ahull till morning when I safely entered Suva Harbour on 31st July. Beryl Turner had air-freighted some more mechanical bits and pieces to me here, the only problem being that the airport was 120 miles away!

After a few days rest in the delightful climate of Fiji, I was on my way once again towards Port Moresby in Papua New Guinea which I reached on the 16th August. On the way, I passed through large areas where a brownish powder was floating on the surface of the water. It turned out that this was fine pumice that had been belched out by an undersea volcano and it was lucky that *Mabel E. Holland*'s engine cooling was of the closed circuit type, as this stuff can cause complete havoc if it finds its way inside an engine.

At Port Moresby I was made most welcome at the yacht club, where John Bray was the secretary. I had an action-packed visit which included a visit to the Highlands to meet the Mud Men, as well as the usual chores of fuelling, watering, maintenance and so on. Then it was on through the Torres Strait to Darwin, half-way point of the circumnavigation, where I had the boat pulled out of the water at Hollands Shipyard for a thorough check-over.

Lifeboats are really designed for short sorties lasting a few hours at a time so it was rather unfair of me to expect everything to work non-stop for up to a month at a time. In general, the lifeboat was remarkably free from mechanical problems apart from the continuing nuisance of leaking prop shaft seals. At Darwin, the shafts were drawn out and after a great deal of discussion and experiment, put back as they had been in the first place. I was greatly helped by the Australian Navy Small Boat Division and by Norman Turner who I had met 'on the airwaves' as he is a 'Ham' radio enthusiast. Another chap named Glen helped by overhauling the steering mechanism which had grown loose from constant use.

As an example of the kind of unnecessary trouble one can run into; when the boat had been put back into the water, an engineer came to service the engines and after he had gone I found that the starboard prop shaft was locked solid. I quite unfairly suspected that he had dropped a spanner into the works but an ex-Royal Navy engineer named Tony Street suggested uncoupling the shaft to see if it was the gearbox or the shaft that was jammed. It turned out to be the latter and as the water was extremely murky due to some underwater blasting in connection with the building of a new quay, there was nothing for it but to have the boat hauled again. As soon as she was out of the water, we saw immediately that the culprit was a large piece of wood that had been forced into the propeller tunnel. A diver could have dealt with it in five minutes if the water had not been so soupy at the time. Darwin had its lighter moments too, however, including some visits to the Royal Navy mess where I had several very friendly evenings including the inauguration of the Royal Navy Association.

With all the maintenance sorted out, I was on my way again on 13 September and enjoyed a fast passage to the next stepping stone in the Indian Ocean, Christmas Island where the mining company very kindly refuelled the boat ready for the long leg to Mauritius. This proved fairly punishing as the wind was at gale force for a total of 13 days. Due to the big sea, I had to keep the boat closed up which made it insufferably hot and humid inside. Shortly after arriving at Port Louis, I was hailed by Betsy Hitz who I had met in Rhode Island in 1976 when she was working for *Cruising World*. She and her husband were taking a sabbatical and they told me a horrific story of being attacked by pirates in the Caribbean when he was badly knifed and they were both lucky to escape with their lives.

I was fortunate in having the name of Christian Wan, Manager of Taylor Smiths Shipyard in Port Louis who turned out to be incredibly helpful and hospitable. Thanks to him a whole host of jobs were done including re-painting the decks which had cracked in the sun and meanwhile he took me to see some of the sights of the island and entertained me to some excellent meals.

The first day of November saw me arrive at Durban where after a short stop I hurried on to Cape Town. The weather around this notorious coast of South Africa was reasonably kind to me and apart from negotiating ships in the fog off Cape Aghulas I was able to make my way to the Cape of Good Hope without much difficulty. Nevertheless this part of the coast always puts me in mind of the painting entitled 'Women and Children First' which portrays officers and men standing to attention on the sloping deck of *HMS Birkenhead* which sank there after hitting a reef. Most of those on board were killed by sharks. Once past the Cape of Good Hope I had to battle my way against the 'Cape Doctor' which is the localised wind blowing off Table Mountain which can reach a speed of 70 knots. Thankfully, things began to calm down after I had reached harbour.

Caroline and Freddie flew out to meet me at Cape Town where we already knew lots of people and could enjoy a few days' holiday. On this occasion it was the skipper rather than the boat that required servicing as I needed to visit the dentist and had developed a lump over one eye. Fortunately this proved to be a non-malignant polyp which was easily dealt with but did force me to remain for several more days than I had originally intended.

FIRST SAIL, NOW POWER

In Cape Town we met Simon Winchester who was sailing around the ocean writing stories about some of the interesting island communities for *The Times* and James Hatfield who was just about to leave on the second leg of his solo circumnavigation. After this pleasant interlude it was on to St Helena where the Governor Dick Baker invited me to Christmas Dinner. He even told a story against himself about how he had fallen into the water when jumping ashore during Prince Andrew's visit to the island. It was not really so surprising as there is no jetty and one has to leap for the steps with the boat heaving up and down in the usual swell.

The next stop was Ascension Island where there is an RAF station that is a vital stepping stone for aircraft making the long flight to The Falklands. Because of the great requirement for fuel a tanker named *Maersk Ascension* is permanently stationed there as a kind of floating filling station while other ships periodically come and fill her up. Her captain, Harry Atkin came bouncing over in an inflatable to wish me a happy New Year which gave me the opportunity to ask if I could refuel from his ship. This, he said, would be no problem at all and he also invited me to make use of an air-conditioned cabin during my stay and have my meals on board. Having, I suppose, a somewhat boring day-to-day routine, he and his crew seemed genuinely pleased to be visited.

Fuelled and watered by *Maersk Ascension*, I set off for Las Palmas, which became a hard slog into the North-east Trades which were blowing strongly that year. I continued after just a couple of days and motored into the depth of the European winter. The temperature fell rapidly as I crossed the Bay of Biscay and it was cold, foggy and rough as I entered the Western Approaches. Thanks to poor radio conditions I was not able to warn my family that I was arriving and finally crept into Plymouth in the dark on the evening of the 31st January to be greeted only by a grumpy docker who tried to make me pay an exorbitant sum for tying up near the entrance to Millbay Dock.

This anti-climatic arrival was soon forgotten when I got ashore and telephoned home and the following day we were all together for a proper celebration. Already the first person to sail round the world singlehanded in both directions, I was now the first to go round singlehanded under power and, of course, the first to do both. The trouble was, I was beginning to have a taste for it and these long ocean passages do give one the opportunity to think about what else remains to be done. I took the boat back to its regular berth at Woodbridge and returned to normal life but in the back of my mind an idea was beginning to form: a singlehanded voyage round the world via the Northwest Passage.

Through Bob Browne, my friend who had been so sea-sick on *Ron Glas* I had struck up a correspondence with the late Captain Tom Pullen, Canada's greatest expert on Arctic navigation. Although quite a number of ships had by this time accomplished the passage, the curious fact was that no British ship had ever left her native shore, passed through the Northwest Passage and returned to Britain. Furthermore no-one of any nationality had succeeded in doing it single-handed. I gradually came round to the idea that this would be a great and worthwhile challenge.

Without doubt it should have been done in a specially-built vessel, preferably made of steel but with the difficulties of finding sponsorship that I had already encountered, it was clear this was beyond my grasp. Therefore, if it was to be accomplished, *Mabel E.Holland* would have to be the vehicle. Though clearly not ideal, I thought she could be modified to improve her resistance to ice at a reasonable cost. Being by now extremely familiar with the boat, I felt I knew all her foibles and felt complete trust in her basic seaworthiness and strength.

The modifications I had in mind were insulation of the cabin areas and strengthening of the hull by adding extra skins of wood using the WEST (Wood Epoxy Saturation Technique) system. I also planned to change the wooden rudder to a metal one and fit new propellers and new seacocks to the heat-exchangers. I had very little time to think about boats during 1985 and it was not until November that *Mabel* was taken out of the water at Whisstocks ready to be stripped down to bare wood and dried out. In January, work began on laminating six layers of 3mm mahogany onto the hull although, surprise! surprise! this took far longer than estimated. Meanwhile my friend John Shallcross, the head of Service Welding Group kindly volunteered to make a new stainless steel rudder, no easy task bearing in mind that the existing shaft was of a different metal and that no distortion of it could be allowed otherwise the bearings would become damaged. I ordered a pair of propellers to be made from a special, and very expensive, bronze alloy under the trade-name 'Superston 70.' The tips of these were to be very much more rounded than the standard ones in the hope that should they come into contact with ice they would not tear or fracture.

Finding financial assistance proved to be very hard work though I did receive several helpful contributions towards my costs. Assistance of a practical kind came from John Shallcross who put one of his men at my disposal to work on the boat with me for nearly a month. Just before departure he made a further generous contribution towards the total fuel costs.

Preparing a boat for a major expedition of this kind is a matter of chasing up a thousand-and-one small jobs and I was driven to frustration by the slow pace of work at Whisstocks. For weeks the job list seemed to become longer rather than shorter and there were all sorts of hold-ups including a major one concerning the main radio transmitter/receiver (see

Chapter 6). Eventually, the work was complete and *Mabel E.Holland* was once more launched into the placid waters of the River Deben from where I moved her to Newcastle for final preparations. Once again time was beginning to be a problem and for this journey, timing was critical because of the very short period during which navigation is possible in the Arctic each year.

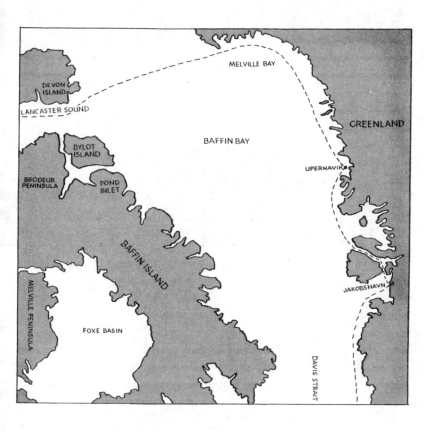

The Northwest Passage, perhaps the most hostile environment
that it is possible to reach by boat

Mabel looking smart prior to launching at Smith's Ship Repairers
before her first circumnavigation

Ocean Bound on her first circumnavigation

The cabin looking forward, showing the single bunk to port and the entrance to the engine room

Additional layers of wood were laminated to the hull to strengthen it against ice

Chart table and instruments

Looking forward in the engine room over the twin Gardner diesels

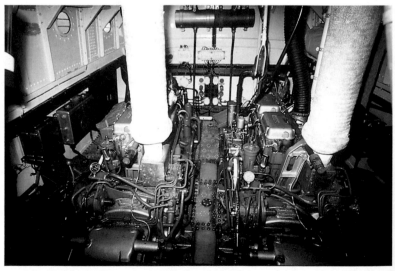

Typical Greenland harbour, complete with ice and fog

Vast cathedrals of ice . . . that are best not approached too
closely in case they decide to topple

The stern cliffs of Devon Island

Following the ice breaker *Des Groseilliers* towards Resolute

Iceberg off the coast of Greenland

Mabel E. Holland seen from the deck of the icebreaker *Des Groseilliers*

No way to treat a boat: *Mabel E. Holland* pushing through heavy ice near Somerset Island

A dramatic archway of ice in Baffin Bay

Resolute, 'capital of the Arctic'. Houses tucked into the hillside
against the weather

The ice-breaker's helicopter drops in for a visit

Mabel E. Holland anchored in front of the Fort Ross huts

Depot Bay: the boat ashore at low tide

Resolute Airport, gateway to the North

Early in the summer, when the sea was still solidly frozen, I made the journey to Fort Ross by skidoo

Impressive pressure ridge in Prince Regent Inlet

The boat solidly frozen in, with bear footprints right over her

The dreadful scene that greeted me when I flew to Fort Ross in August 1987: *Mabel E. Holland* lying awash in the shallows of Depot Bay

Mabel E. Holland on the foreshore at Depot Bay with fuel cans unloaded to lighten her

I pitched my tent on the rocky shore of Depot Bay

The author with a Twin Otter, invaluable flying workhorse of the Arctic

Fort Ross from the air, with *Mabel E. Holland* just visible in the centre of the picture

We built a small cairn of rocks and named it 'Point Mabel'

Polar bear having a good sniff around my fuel dump

. . . picked up a 70lb kitbag as if it were a toy

I had to take exception when he began biting the dinghy

Easy when you know how. Built within an hour, this 'instant igloo' provides far better shelter than a tent

Pulling a 20-ton lifeboat out of the water on an arctic beach several hundred miles from the nearest civilization, proved no mean task

Inching to safety, *Mabel* is dragged up the slope over greased timbers

Two electric winches hauling on six-part purchases finally succeeded in dragging *Mabel* clear of the water

Rugged exterior concealing a heart of gold: marine biologist Buster Welsh proved a tower of strength when it looked as if my expedition might fail

The Honda trike and trailer which carried our heavy equipment from the airstrip at Fort Ross to the boat

Working on the bottom, with distinctly limited headroom

My arctic boatyard, showing the less-than-ideal working conditions

Sorting out equipment on deck prior to relaunching the boat at
Depot Bay

Mabel E. Holland anchored at Depot Bay

Caroline came to help me repair the boat in 1988 and fell in love with the Arctic

The two huts at Fort Ross were built by the Hudson's Bay Company and remained as refugees after the trading post was abandoned

The face that appeared at the window one breakfast-time, which I snapped with the last frame on my roll of film

Inside one of the refuge huts at Fort Ross

Fishing for Arctic Char is a special annual treat at Cresswell Bay

Ice expert Captain Tom Pullen and his wife Kitty pose with Captain Heinz Aye and myself on the bridge of the cruise ship *Society Explorer*

Motoring along the narrow gap between ice-floes and the shore
became a matter of course

Passing John Bockstoce's *Belvedere* near Cape Francis

To lift the boat out at Inuvik, I had to improvise slings from a
cats-cradle of her own warps

Mabel E. Holland being lifted out of the Mackenzie River by the
container lift at Inuvik freight debot

Working on the boat at Inuvik; well-dressed against dust, heat and mosquitos

Underneath the lifeboat, showing the rubbing strips which made it so difficult to sand off the paint properly

Rick Thomas (blue T-shirt) and crew on the deck of *Northanger*. First Briton through the Northwest Passage by a few hours, he was killed shortly afterwards in a climbing accident

The boat repainted and ready for launching at Inuvik

Once a gathering-point for the whaling fleets, Herschel Island is now a nature reserve

Some of the buildings which are being restored at Herschel Island

Point Barrow, the unimpressive headland which is the most
northerly point of Alaska

The fog cleared to reveal the dramatic snow-capped mountains of
the Aleutians

Alongside a ship which gave me fuel at Port Moresby

Heavy going in the Indian Ocean

'Here comes that Pommie lifeboat again'. At remote Bramble Cay I found the same fishermen that I had met on my previous circumnavigation

Mabel E. Holland under her protective covering of 'shade cloth' at Darwin

Dramatic sea which built up in a few minutes in the Aghulas Current

A flotilla of yachts escorted me up the River Tyne

Chapter 5

The First Year

I AM SURE that any long-distance voyager will tell you that actually leaving comes as a relief. As the appointed day approaches, one becomes increasingly frantic trying to cope with all the last-minute jobs which never seem to become fewer. Car loads of food, clothing and equipment of every sort have to be stowed, charts and documents checked, fuelling and watering arranged, letters written, officials seen and so on. On top of this I had to put my business in order and make sure that all was well at home before I could finally go aboard *Mabel E.Holland* on the morning of July 14, 1986.

We drove down to Albert Edward Dock near the mouth of the Tyne where I had left the boat. *Mabel* looked absurdly small against the shipping and factories of the Tyne and perilously low in the water under her heavy load of fuel and stores. The bright orange paintwork of the superstructure also gave her a somewhat toy-like appearance against the drab background of the dock. A small group of friends and supporters had gathered, together with a TV news crew to ensure that we all felt thoroughly self-conscious as we said our goodbyes.

I started up the faithful Gardner diesels that had already driven me round the globe once, cast off the lines and with much cheerful waving set off to sea. It was a warm, sunny and almost windless day – perfect to let me to find my sea-legs and tidy up the boat. The famous annual Tall Ships Race fleet was due in the Tyne but sadly I was leaving the day before they arrived so I missed the treat of seeing them.

Feeling pretty weary from all the last-minute rush, I thought it would be a smart idea to have a good night's sleep so I decided to pop into the small harbour of Amble on the Northumberland coast for a few quiet hours before going into battle with the North Sea. In fact, when I crept out of harbour early next morning the sea was still virtually flat calm but a thick fog had rolled in, obliging me to keep a constant watch as *Mabel* rolled steadily along on a Northerly heading for Aberdeen.

People often ask how I manage to adapt from a 'normal' way of life ashore to one of solitude on board. I think that they imagine me just sitting there in the wheelhouse with no-one to speak to and nothing to do except feel lonely. In reality one is so busy, especially at the outset of a voyage, that time passes quickly. Navigation, house-keeping and attending to the boat fills one's day with an endless succession of small tasks. It is important to settle down into a routine as soon as possible. I always try to eat meals at regular times and not to put off today's jobs to tomorrow. You need to build up this discipline when things are easy so that you can really cling on to it when the going gets tough. When one is cold, wet and utterly weary it is fatally easy to just let things drift and so lose control of the situation.

There was a long-standing arrangement to call at Aberdeen because the whisky distillers Grants had very kindly donated £1,000 and wanted to take a picture of me receiving a case of their famous product, a request that I was very ready to fall in with. In any case, the weather was now beginning to deteriorate quite rapidly with forecasts of gales so Aberdeen seemed an excellent idea especially as I knew Caroline was going to drive up with Freddie and my nephew Nicholas for a 'final, final' goodbye. With the case of Scotch safely stowed away below, we had a jolly meal ashore before Caroline and the boys headed south. After 48 hours the weather had calmed down sufficiently to let me set off again towards Peterhead before striking out across the Moray Firth to John O' Groat's.

After anchoring briefly at Thurso for a rest, I coast-hopped along the North Coast of Scotland as far as Loch Eriboll, a convenient bolt-hole just short of Cape Wrath, which was to be my jumping-off point into the Atlantic. It was now blowing hard again and I waited there for a further 48 hours, hoping the weather would calm down a bit but since it showed no signs of doing so I grew impatient and decided to press on. I can only describe the nine-day crossing to Cape Farewell, the southern tip of Greenland as rough. The wind was never less than Force 6 and often up to Force 8 from between south-west and north-west. It was heavy going.

Deeply laden with fuel and stores, *Mabel* ploughed steadily along at 6 knots taking the waves green over her bows. Perhaps this is a good moment to explain that although she is a lifeboat and therefore just about as seaworthy as a boat of that size can be, *Mabel* is far wetter and gives an infinitely more tiring ride than a sailing yacht such as *Ocean Bound*. Without sails to steady her, she rolls and corkscrews incessantly and, due to her weight, punches through the tops of waves rather than riding over them. In heavy weather, spray constantly dashes against the wheelhouse windows while solid water pours along the decks before cascading back into the sea amidships. I have to stay 'indoors' virtually the whole time and even when sitting on the saddle seat behind the wheel, it is necessary to hang on, to avoid being thrown from side to side.

It is easy to forget how far north the top of Scotland is. From Cape Wrath I needed to make only about another 60 miles of northing to reach latitude 60N which runs through the Shetland Islands and also touches Cape Farewell. If it were not for the Gulf Stream, the Shetlands would be covered in ice like Greenland. The weather worked itself up into a frenzy in time for my arrival at Cape Farewell which I rounded at dusk in the teeth of a screaming Force 9-10 Westerly. When daylight returned, I had my first sight of ice. To begin with, this consisted of small 'growlers'; chunks of old ice that have broken off larger floes and float along with most of their bulk hidden below the surface. In spite of their small size they are just as dangerous as the full-sized variety, especially in bad weather. It does not take much imagination to foresee the result of a wooden vessel falling off a steep wave and smashing into a block of granite-hard ice weighing several hundred tons.

At this time of year there is about five hours of darkness per night and as I was so apprehensive about the risk of hitting a 'growler' I would stop the engines and lie ahull for the darkest hours. This also gave me the chance to prepare some hot food and snatch some sleep without too much worry. One would not do this in an area of busy shipping but fortunately there is very little in this part of the world.

From Cape Farewell I turned north and began to follow the coast of Greenland. The Pilot book defines the Northwest Passage as beginning at the Davis Strait, between Greenland and Baffin Island, and ending at the Bering Strait so as I passed Latitude 63N I felt that at last my great adventure was properly under way. It took the early explorers a long time to realize that the centre of Baffin Bay is nearly always choked with pack-ice even in summer and that it is useless trying to sail straight across. The way to reach Lancaster Sound is to follow the Greenland coast right up to Melville Bay and then cross over through what the old whalers called the 'North Water' to the Canadian side.

To begin with at least, there was a wide channel between the ice and the Greenland coast and I was able to keep about 20 miles offshore on my way up to my intended stopping point at Jacobshavn. The amount of ice in the water steadily increased, becoming a mushy soup of partly-melted sea-ice with harder lumps of old ice mixed in.

Up to this point, I had been able to use the autopilot to take care of the steering but now the compass, which controls it, began to grow more and more sluggish as we sailed north. The magnetic North Pole is actually on Bathurst Island, not far from the settlement of Resolute, towards which I was heading and if you take a magnetic compass needle there, it will try to point straight up and down. The nearer you sail to the magnetic pole, the weaker the directional force becomes and the greater the Magnetic Variation, the difference in angle between the magnetic and geographic poles. As I approached Jacobshavn, I was already having to apply a grotesque 50 degrees of variation when laying off a course and I watched with some alarm as the compass card swung lazily through a huge angle as *Mabel* rolled along.

Actually knowing the ship's position was not a problem thanks to a magical-seeming piece of electronics called 'Sat-Nav'. Receiving signals from the Transit series of orbiting satellites, this gives a lat. and long. position accurate to within a mile or so at intervals of around one hour. With daylight and good visibility it is reasonably easy to steer a course by reference to the sun, the direction of the waves or any land that may be in sight but the curse of arctic navigation is fog which dropped like a cold, soggy blanket when I was still about five miles from Jacobshavn, feeling my way through increasingly thick ice. To add to my problems it was getting dark.

The first thing I had to learn about sea ice was that it does not remain in one place but is pushed around by wind and current. That is why ice conditions can change so rapidly and why in the past so many ships got trapped when the ice suddenly closed in on them. On this occasion, north-westerly winds had pushed the loose ice against the Greenland coast around Jacobshavn, mingling with icebergs calved from the massive glaciers that come down to the sea near there.

This was the first occasion on which I had needed to push the boat through real pack-ice and it was not an especially pleasant experience. Looking back with hindsight, it was as nothing compared to the ice I was to encounter later on but at the time it seemed dreadfully unfair to the poor old boat to keep the throttles open while she slowly forged ahead through the mushy pack, accompanied by disagreeable squealing, crunching and grinding sounds. It turned out that I must have struck some especially hard and sharp-edged pieces of ice because I found that the hull had been scored to a depth of nearly three-quarters of an inch at one point. Not a very encouraging first experience with ice.

After three hours of this I thought I could see a faint darkening of the fog indicating the headland that marked the entrance to Jacobshavn and I continued round it to find the smeary lights of the harbour appearing through the gloom. It was full of pack-ice and small growlers but I managed to force a way through until I could make fast alongside a pair of Danish ice patrol boats. It was 4.30 in the morning on August 5 and the first stage of the journey was over.

The purpose of my visit to Jacobshavn was to refuel but I eventually stayed for three days hoping that the weather would improve and the ice disperse. If I had been dreaming of tucking into a delicious meal in a cosy restaurant then it had to remain a dream as it is an austere little settlement with no public eating place. One of the Ice Patrol vessels allowed me to use their shower and wash some clothes but I continued to eat on board. In the brief periods when it was not foggy I looked around this lonely little community. The inhabitants of these northern settlements prefer to be called Inuit which in their language means 'The People'. The term Eskimo means 'Eater of raw meat' and is the insulting name given to them by Indians who were their enemies in the past. They are friendly and curious but rather strange in their manner. Unfortunately, nature has not equipped them to metabolize alcohol in the same way as the Europeans so they become intoxicated easily. Alcoholism is a permanent problem in the Arctic.

Jacobshavn is sheltered by a large island named Disko and after leaving harbour I set off up the Vaigat, the narrow strait between Disko and Greenland. One of Greenland's massive glaciers comes down to the sea here and calves huge, impressive icebergs the size of cathedrals. Unlike the sneaky growlers, there is no danger of failing to see one of these massive and really rather beautiful chunks of bluish freshwater ice but the temptation to venture too close to them needs to be resisted. As the part that is in the sea gradually melts, the berg becomes unstable until it finally topples over with a mighty roar, sending up huge waves. Early voyagers often wrote of the terrifying noise and violence that results when a big berg, drifting along on the current, hits floes that are attached to the shore. I never witnessed this and tried to keep a respectful distance away from bergs but seeing one capsize from a distance was quite impressive enough.

After a further brief stop at the tiny settlement of Upernavik, I set off on the potentially tricky passage to Lancaster Sound. Reports that I had collected at Jacobshavn indicated that there was reasonably clear water for about 15 miles offshore which is rather better than average. When Willy de Roos was here in 1977, in company with the Canadian yacht *J.E.Bernier II* he found considerable difficulty in getting past Melville Bay but conversely had a relatively easy passage later on. My experience was the exact opposite. Sailing north as far as latitude 75N, I then set off in a gentle curve across the top of Baffin Bay, finding open water all the way. From about two hundred miles east of Lancaster Sound I finally lost the use of the autopilot and as I came into the Sound the compass itself ceased to make any sense.

The great difficulty of navigating in this area single-handed is the need to keep a constant lookout in case one should crash into ice inadvertently. Without the autopilot, I was forced to spend up to 18 hours per day steering by hand with occasional snatched meals and quick sessions at the chart table. The question was, how to rest? I decided that the only thing to do was shut down the engines and let the boat drift in the hope that she would do so in the same direction and at roughly the same speed as the bergs. I timed my rests to coincide with the brief period of darkness and slept fitfully, dreaming about monstrous icebergs. The sea is deep right up to the land which is usually high and rugged so there is no possibility of anchoring.

I caught sight of Devon Island at the same time as a north-westerly gale began to blow and as I was fearful of approaching the land in bad weather, I once more stopped the engines and lay-to for 12 hours until conditions eased some-what. Though desolate and forbidding, the headlands of Devon Island are strangely beautiful. The cliffs rise sheer out of the water to a height of around 90m (300ft) and are topped with a permanent ice-cap. The waters of Lancaster Sound are particularly rich in plankton which provides the basic food for an extensive chain of wildlife – fish, birds and mammals such as deer, foxes and bears. Far from being a dead area, it is teeming with wildlife.

Lighter winds brought fog but fortunately Lancaster Sound is deep right to the shore and I was able to cruise carefully along within sight of the steep, grey cliffs. By August 16, just over a month after leaving the Tyne, I reached Beechy

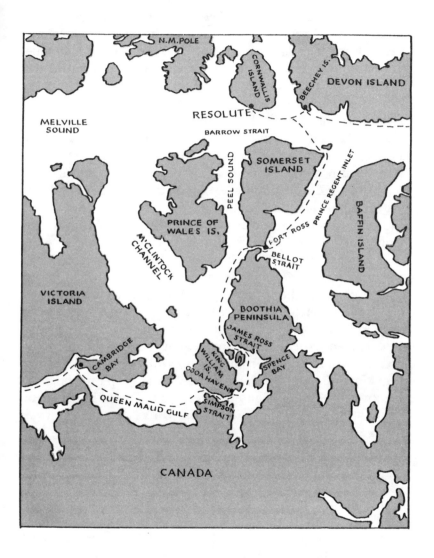

Island, a gloomy, featureless lump of land on which lie the graves of three Victorian seamen who died and were buried there in 1846 during the early stages of the disastrous Franklin expedition (see Chapter 1). It was in 1984 that the Canadian scientist Dr Owen Beattie exhumed these bodies and discovered that they contained high levels of lead, presumably from the tinned meat which was a staple part of their diet. Dr Beattie's conclusion is that on top of all their other problems Franklin's men were gradually going demented through lead poisoning and that by the time they abandoned their ships they were not making rational decisions. However, another scientist Dr Jim Savelle believes that Beattie has overplayed the lead-poisoning aspect though it is perfectly true that the Franklin expedition seems to have suffered far more deaths from illness than other contemporary expeditions.

When I turned into the Bay at Beechey Island, I was surprised to see two ships alongside each other at anchor, one a tanker and the other the Canadian icebreaker *Des Groseilliers*, named after the French woodsman who helped to found the Hudson's Bay Company when he went there in 1668 on an expedition sponsored by Charles II. The icebreaker was refuelling from the tanker. Having hardly seen a ship since leaving Scotland, other than the patrol boats at Jacobshavn, I was delighted to receive an invitation to go on board after I called up the icebreaker on VHF radio. As it was reasonably calm, I took *Mabel E. Holland* alongside and climbed aboard.

On board, I was given an open-hearted welcome by Captain Claude Guimont who plied me with food and drink and wanted to hear all about this lone Englishman who had appeared out of nowhere in an old lifeboat. Actually, they did know I was in the area because I had written to the Canadian authorities well before leaving England. Tom Pullen had been to see me and had inspected the boat in order to give a report to the Canadian Coastguard. I also met Larry Solar who was the 'Ice Observer' aboard and he was an absolute mine of information on everything to do with ice conditions. I got on with both these men extremely well and they could not have been more friendly or welcoming. In all I spent about five hours on board during which time I was dined in style, able to have a hot shower and wash some clothes.

In spite of their friendliness, the story that I received from Guimont and Solar was far from encouraging. It was beginning to become clear that I had chosen the wrong year to make an attempt on the Northwest Passage. Average temperatures during July and August had been two or three degrees lower than normal with the result that the ice in Peel Sound, Franklin Strait and James Ross Strait showed no signs of melting and that even the channel to Resolute was still packed with nine-tenths ice. This was all rather depressing but I remembered that Tom Pullen frequently emphasized that conditions can change very quickly. A week of good weather might well result in a dramatic change. 'Good weather' in this instance would mean storm force winds that would crack the ice and pile it up in one particular quarter leaving clear water elsewhere. Calm weather would not help.

I also felt that however friendly these seafarers were personally, at an official level the Canadian Coastguard was bound to take a fairly jaundiced view of lone yachtsmen setting off into the Arctic, on the grounds that sooner or later they might be asked to rescue them. During the coming days I learned to recognize when I was receiving an 'Ottawa reply' which was normally that I should not take risks that might cause the Canadian Government trouble or expense or a 'personal reply' from individual Coastguard officers which was more likely to be 'We will help you if we can.'

For instance, Guimont told me that in a few hours, after refuelling was complete, *Des Groseilliers* would be setting off for Resolute where I also wished to go. If they encountered me on the way, they would be happy to provide an escort but needed to obtain official approval first. With his help I therefore concocted a signal to Ottawa saying that I needed to reach Resolute in order to make repairs and requested ice-breaker assistance. I had already decided to make every effort to make it to Resolute because if I did decide to give up for the time being, that would be the obvious place to leave the boat.

They also agreed to sell me some diesel which I could take directly from a hose. This was going to be a lot easier than ferrying it from the shore in cans so I accepted gladly and topped off the main tanks. Then after saying *au revoir* to these useful new friends I set off. From Beechey Island, it is a 60 mile crossing to Resolute on the southern shore of Cornwallis Island and as it was still foggy and the compass was totally useless, navigation was a problem. Not having either radar or gyro compass, the only thing I could do was keep the wind in the same quarter and hope for the best.

Since the wind was from the north-east I hoped that this would push the ice to the south and create a passage but I soon found that this was over-optimistic. I had only gone about five miles before the ice thickened to five tenths and soon afterwards it became virtually solid. Even with full throttle I was making virtually no progress so I had no alternative but to stop and wait. I was also slightly apprehensive about a polar bear which was making its way towards me across the ice, obviously curious about this strange-looking craft. The bear received the shock of its life when, to my great relief, *Des Groseilliers* appeared astern with an 'I told you so' look about her and called me up on the VHF. 'Did I want an escort to Resolute?' they asked. Did I ever!

Captain Guimont explained that I was to position *Mabel E.Holland* as close to their stern as I possibly could, in order to remain in the small 'vee' of open water she created as she forced her way through the ice. The way that modern ice-breakers work is by riding up over the ice with their sloping bow whereupon the ship's weight breaks the ice and the hull is able to shove it aside. The ice then grinds noisily along the ship's reinforced steel sides before coming together again after it has passed. Another less powerful ship can make its way along the channel of broken ice so created but the individual chunks are still too heavy for a small vessel such as *Mabel* to cope with, hence the need to stay so close.

I soon found out that when they said 'close' they meant virtually touching the stern of *Des Groseilliers*. This was a most uncomfortable situation with the water boiling up from the icebreakers' powerful screws and large pieces of ice whacking into our sides or coming up from below. With the two Gardners thundering away on full power, we were making about 2 knots and it called for a lot of skill and patience on the part of the officers of *Des Groseilliers* to match their speed to mine. In normal conditions, *Mabel E.Holland* can reach her 'hull speed' of around 8 knots with power in hand. It was now that I really began to feel that all the time and effort of reinforcing the hull had not been wasted. As the ice clonked and rumbled along her sides I thought about those expensive Superston propellers smashing away at it and of the fantastic strength and reliability that the RNLI specified for their gearboxes and drive shafts which enabled them to survive the brutal shocks as the props hit solid ice.

In this somewhat nerve-racking fashion, our little convoy made its way towards Resolute, the so-called 'Capital of the Arctic.' I am not sure what I was really expecting to find but Resolute is a fairly bleak little settlement by any standards, consisting of an untidy scatter of brightly-painted houses dotted about on a sloping shore above the bay, with a collection of oil-storage tanks as the main feature. The real focus of activity is around the airport, five miles away, from which there are jet services to Edmonton about twice a week. There is no harbour as such and no jetty or crane and if they want to bring a boat out of the water they just drag it up the shale beach with a bulldozer. When we arrived, the bay was full of pack-ice so after finding what seemed a suitable spot I had to find a hole to drop the anchor through. Subsequently I was to learn that anchoring in these circumstances is a somewhat academic exercise: if the boat is in pack-ice it cannot drift away but on the other hand if the ice decides to move it will take the boat with it, anchor and all!

Very tired after the passage from Beechey Island I had a meal followed by my first proper sleep for a number of days before thinking about going ashore. On the morning of 19 August I inflated my Tinker Traveller dinghy and prepared to row ashore. This proved to be no easy task, pushing through the mushy ice with many larger lumps in it. After reaching the beach, I found my way to the Royal Canadian Mounted Police post in order to register my arrival in Canada. Of course, they knew all about me already and I began to realize that the Arctic, in spite of its vast empty spaces, is really like a spread-out village. There are so few people that the 'Mounties' know who everyone is and roughly where to find them at any one moment. Virtually everyone in Resolute seemed to know who I was before I had even stepped ashore! Certainly, I received the most extraordinary welcome from people at Resolute who were never too busy to drop whatever they were doing and help me find whatever I was looking for at the time.

The first thing to find was the airport and I had no difficulty hitching a lift in a pickup truck which bounced along the dusty, unmade road to the 'North Camp'; a collection of depots, offices and workshops clustered alongside the runway which is the life-line and the real *raison d'etre* of the whole place. I wondered what the industry of Resolute could be and slowly came to understand that there isn't one. Beginning with an Inuit community, Resolute has gradually grown into a cluster of service industries, all looking after each other. Exploration and survey are the only really outward-looking activities apart from which there are the Royal Canadian Mounted Police, the airport workers, the maintenance and supply workers and so on, all to keep the little community ticking over. In addition to the jet service from Edmonton smaller 'bush' aircraft fan out from Resolute to supply smaller settlements.

The main reason for calling at the airport was to collect a package containing a special piece of cable for my high-frequency radio set. The story of this radio was a complete saga in itself. For my previous circumnavigation in *Mabel*, I had managed to obtain the loan of a military radio transmitter/receiver from Plessey. This was smaller and more rugged than the usual 400 Watt marine sets and suited the boat very well so in January 1986 I again approached the Plessey people who kindly agreed to let me have the same set.

In a large company like this, it seems as if there is great difficulty in getting one department to communicate with another. It was agreed that the set would work better with a whip aerial and that Plessey's would install it. At the time the boat was at Woodbridge, only an hour's drive from the Plessey factory and in April an engineer came to measure up for this new aerial. Thereafter, in spite of frequent reminders, no-one arrived to install it which was especially irksome as it stopped me from completing work on insulating the interior.

In the middle of June, I moved the boat to Newcastle where she was to be loaded up and thereafter redoubled my entreaties to Plessey to install the radio and its new aerial. Finally at the beginning of July when I was nearly ready to go, two men came all the way up from Ilford to Newcastle to install the set. This was not easy because the boat was now at a dock where there is no electricity or workshop so jobs that could have been cleared up in a few minutes at the boatyard in Woodbridge, required hours of driving around searching for tools or getting brackets made up.

Later, when I was half way across the Atlantic, I realized that a vital cable connecting the special charging unit to the special batteries was missing and that as it was a military fitting it was not the sort of thing I could improvise with a bent paper-clip and a blob of solder. On reaching Jacobshavn, I had to telephone to England in order to have this essential bit of equipment sent to me at Resolute but when I finally caught up with it there, I found that my troubles were still far from over. The customs declaration on the package said 'Radio equipment' which seemed to send the Royal Canadian Mounted Police into a frenzy. Although they fill the role of Customs in this part of the world, they explained that they are not clearance agents and that this should have been done in Montreal. In vain I explained that all my package contained was a short length of cable with special jack plugs on either end. Finally they released the package, with ill grace.

When I eventually got the radio charged up, it turned out there was also an intermittent fault on the transmission side and the end result of all this was that I was going to set off into one of the most dangerous sea areas of the world without a reliable long-range radio.

After all this excitement at the airport I hitched back to the 'South Camp' just in time to see *Mabel* quietly drifting out to sea. The wind had changed and the pack was slowly moving out of the bay, taking the boat with it. I leapt into the dinghy and set off in pursuit, reaching her just in time before getting into uncomfortably rough and dangerous water. The anchor, which had been dragged remorselessly along the bottom was recovered and I motored back into the bay which was at least freer of ice now.

My next call ashore was to the Ice Patrol Centre where I hoped to receive some cheerful news about ice conditions in Peel Sound, the route I expected to take south towards Franklin Strait but their reports were as gloomy as Larry Solar's had been on board *Des Groseilliers*. Though I called on them every day for the next 12 days the story was always the same – no change, no channel open in Peel Sound. This was beginning to be depressing. The sailing 'season' was rapidly coming to its end before it had even begun and I was forced to bend my thoughts to the possibility of having *Mabel E.Holland* pulled out of the water at Resolute and calling the whole thing off for a year. I was very reluctant to consider this because although I had been on the move for a little over a month, the major part of the Northwest Passage still lay ahead.

After a few days, the annual supply ship arrived and as she prepared to unload the wind began to rise rapidly until it reached an alarming 65 knots with driving snow. This pushed ice back into the bay and I spent a most uncomfortable 15 hours constantly moving the boat and re-anchoring in order to avoid becoming trapped and driven ashore by the pack.

Before I got too restless, my routine was interrupted by the arrival of the cruise ship *World Discoverer*, her dark blue hull dramatically crusted with ice from the freezing spray. She is something very unusual, an ice-strengthened passenger ship which makes cruises to the Arctic and Antarctic so that the customers can enjoy the savage beauty of the scenery and the wildlife without leaving the luxury of a five-star hotel. The first passenger ship to pass through the Northwest Passage was the *Lindblad Explorer* in 1984 and then *World Discoverer* went through from west to east in 1985. On this occasion she had picked up a fresh load of passengers in Greenland and was intending to sail through the Passage and then continue to Tahiti.

Tom Pullen, who was the on-board Ice Pilot, had told me the ship would be coming and this was one reason for waiting at Resolute. I went on board to meet the Captain and to parley with my friend and adviser Pullen. In addition to the *Des Groseilliers* which I had followed, there was a second icebreaker at Resolute, the *Pierre Radisson* and so the captains and ice-pilots of all three ships, plus the Ice Patrol Service officer stationed at Resolute, went into conference to decide what *World Discoverer* should do. Basically, the Canadians all said that the ship would not get through that year but her Captain, Heinz Aye, was very reluctant to give up without a fight. He had 120 passengers on board who were paying a lot of money to be taken through the Northwest Passage and he felt that he could not simply turn round and retreat unless it had been clearly shown that the trip was impossible. Although ready to go along with this, Pullen was pretty sanguine about their chances and privately showed me the latest aerial survey reports. Ice was still reported as ten-tenths in Peel Sound, Franklin Strait and James Ross Strait with lots of huge floes made of multi-year ice which is far harder and stronger than first-year ice.

Between them the captains evolved the following plan: *World Discoverer* would back-track as far as Beechey Island before turning south and making her way down Prince Regent Inlet as far as Bellot Strait. The thinking behind this was that Prince Regent Inlet, being sheltered from the prevailing north-westerly drift of ice, normally offers easier conditions than Peel Sound which runs down the other side of Somerset Island. The narrow Bellot Strait separates Somerset Island from the long finger of Boothia Peninsular and offers a short-cut route from the Prince Regent side to the Peel Sound side. *World Discoverer* would attempt to break through Bellot Strait where she would rendezvous with the icebreaker *Pierre Radisson*. I could not understand why the icebreaker and the liner did not travel together but Tom Pullen told me that the icebreaker could get along better if it went at full speed and made 'a clean cut' through the heavy pack. Also, if they positioned themselves at the western exit to Bellot Strait they would be better placed to judge if it were possible to continue further. As it turned out, the ice in Peel Sound was formidable and *Pierre Radisson* had great difficulty in breaking through. Tom was more optimistic than the other experts and emphasized that things could change dramatically after a few days of strong wind.

Anyway, I thought that I could benefit from all this activity and to a certain extent 'tag along' with it. There was plenty of time later to reflect on whether this was over-ambitious in view of all the gloom and doom that the Ice Patrol predicted but at the time I felt that I should not miss any opportunity to press on. Sub-consciously, I suppose I thought that with a Canadian Coastguard icebreaker and a cruise liner in the same area, they would not simply abandon me to my fate if the worst came to the worst. As things turned out, this was perhaps a little complacent as the Arctic had only just begun to show what a hostile environment it can be. With hindsight I would have saved myself a lot of trouble by having the boat pulled out at Resolute and leaving her there till the following year.

My plan was to set off ahead of the liner in the hope of getting to Bellot Strait at roughly the same time. They were going to stay for a full day of sight-seeing so after the conference was complete I went back to *Mabel E. Holland* and got under way immediately, glad to be on the move again after 12 days kicking my heels in Resolute.

To begin with things went rather well. Visibility was fairly good and with a north-westerly wind of 20 knots push-ing the ice away from the coast of Cornwallis Island, sea conditions were reasonable. I made good progress until the evening when I was off the south-west tip of the Island and hove-to for a rest during the hours of darkness. When I awoke it was becoming foggy so I set off again using the wind direction as the only directional reference. The visibility kept deteriorating and it was very easy to become disoriented especially as I had been hand-steering for so many hours. I had hoped to find Cape Clarence, the north-east corner of Somerset Island, before darkness came again but although I

105

knew from the SatNav that I was near it, I could not catch sight of it in time.

With a rising north-easterly wind and poor visibility, I was taken by surprise when we motored straight into nine-tenths pack-ice that brought the boat rapidly to a standstill. The sea grew calmer because there was now ice to windward but with every minute that passed more and more of it came pressing in making it impossible to escape. I was now totally disorientated and had no idea which direction to head in so there was nothing for it but to stop engines and let the ice take the initiative. Now that it was nearing the end of August, the luxury of almost permanent daylight was fast disappearing. It was foggy, darkness was falling and we were completely surrounded by impenetrable ice.

There was absolutely nothing that I could do except sit and wait. The ice was not still but heaving on the swell so that the floes made an ugly noise as they ground against each other and the hull of *Mabel E.Holland* which groaned in reply. It was altogether not a pleasant situation and I thought of all the experienced ice-observers who had shaken their heads and said 'You won't get through.' Leaving the wheelhouse, I went forward to the little fore-cabin and prepared some hot food. For once I could eat it at leisure for there was absolutely nothing I could do except sit there and listen to the eerie sounds of the ice. When the engines are running, they give a certain amount of warmth to the wheelhouse but without them the interior of the boat soon became icy. The air temperature was well below zero and new ice was beginning to form on the sea. I got into my bunk and dozed fitfully.

When daylight returned, I found that the boat was surrounded by ice as far as the eye could see and it was far too heavy to be able to push the boat through it. I began to feel thoroughly scared and wondered how I was going to find a way out of this situation. But then, in a classic display of Arctic caprice, the wind went round to the Northwest and began to take the pressure off the ice so that after a few hours, leads appeared along which I could make my way back towards Resolute. Having more or less settled on this course of action I decided for some reason to call up *World Discoverer* on the radio and to my great surprise got through as the set decided to work for once.

I spoke to Tom Pullen who as usual was very positive. His opinion, correct as it turned out, was that a lead would open up along the east side of Somerset Island so rather against my better judgement I agreed to turn round and have another crack at it. In the late afternoon, therefore, I re-entered the pack but although there were open leads to begin with, they soon closed up and as night fell I was in a similar predicament to the previous night and kicked myself for not continuing to Resolute when it was still possible. There was nothing for it but to stop engines and heave-to, as before. I was worrying about the time factor as I imagined that *World Discoverer* would be on her way by now, would pass by without seeing me and go rushing on to Bellot Strait while I was still stuck at the very beginning of Prince Regent Inlet.

When it was light next morning, I clambered on top of the wheelhouse for a look round with the binoculars and to my great excitement I could see Somerset Island and near it a black streak of water along the shore. It appeared to be about two miles away to the west and it was obvious I must make every effort to reach it. Doing so took six hours of nerve-jarring effort. Abusing the poor old boat no end, I just left the throttles fully open and let her slowly force her way through at about half a knot.

The punishment to the hull was terrible; it was like deliberately ramming the boat into a pile of bricks, again and again. Without the extra layers of wood and epoxy, the special propellers and the steel rudder, *Mabel* would never have survived. As it was, she creaked and groaned and protested with every joint but kept moving slowly forward. The strain on the rudder damaged the steering gear which I had to fix later on. As we battered our way slowly towards the open water, I felt that it was also moving towards us. In fact, the wind had turned to the West and was pushing the ice away from the shore which was exactly what I needed, so it was with an enormous feeling of relief that we finally broke through and I felt the boat leap forward as she escaped from the icy embrace of the pack.

The open water extended for a scant 200 yards or so from the shore but I was beginning to learn that this much water was a luxury. I had also learned the hard way that it is vital to stay as close as possible to the shore because big pieces of ice would go aground before they can hit you. This narrow channel continued the whole way down the Somerset Island shore and I pushed on down it as fast as I could for 120 miles, passing the tiny settlement of Cresswell Bay *en route*. Four days after leaving Resolute, I arrived at Fort Ross, at the entrance to Bellot Strait and was greatly surprised to find that I had beaten *World Discoverer* to it.

Despite its impressive name, Fort Ross is an abandoned Hudson's Bay Company post consisting of just two wooden huts but it is nevertheless a place with considerable history. It was near here that M'Clintock spent a year in the steam yacht *Fox* during which time he finally cleared up the mystery of what had happened to the Franklin expedition. Little did I realize how well I was to come to know it.

Anchoring about 100 yards off, I inflated the dinghy and went ashore to investigate. I found that one of the huts had been vandalized by polar bears. The other was intact and bore the signs of having been used for shelter by hunters and scientists from time to time. It had an oil heater that looked as if it could be made to work. It was nice to be on dry land after the stress of the previous four days and I spent some time looking around the area before returning on board for the rare pleasure of an uninterrupted sleep.

108

Early next morning I heard the blare of a fog-horn and stuck my head out of the hatch to find *World Discoverer* just coming to anchor a short distance away. By now the passengers knew all about *Mabel E.Holland* and our progress was obviously a talking point on board and as it was about 8am the ship's inflatable came bouncing over to invite me to breakfast! It was quite disconcerting to feel at one moment totally alone in the vast wastes of the Arctic and at the next be whisked into the centrally-heated comfort of the ship where I was surrounded by lots of friendly people asking questions while stewards in white jackets brought a cooked breakfast of the kind I could only dream about aboard *Mabel E.Holland*.

The reason I had got to Fort Ross first was that the ship had taken a 'scenic route' which involved crossing the centre of Prince Regent Inlet. The ice had been a lot thicker than the satellite photos suggested and she had difficulty in getting through. At the same time, even the powerful icebreaker *Pierre Radisson* had only managed to make her way down Peel Sound – the other side of the Island – with difficulty. I learned this when the icebreaker's captain and ice-pilot suddenly appeared over the mountains in the small helicopter that the ship carries. What the early discoverers would not have given for such a magic carpet, I thought!

The two officers were the bearers of bad news. They had not come to see me but the captain of *World Discoverer* in order to persuade him to abandon the idea of going through Bellot Strait. The ice on the Franklin Strait side was much too thick, they said and they even took him up in the helicopter to see for himself. Once again, Captain Aye refused to be put off. He would not turn back until he could make no further progress. After a lot of tutting and head-shaking, it was agreed the icebreaker would stay put until the *World Discoverer* had made her effort to progress beyond Bellot Strait.

I was told in no uncertain terms that I must not try to follow as they were talking about heavy ice under pressure which would crush my small wooden boat like an egg if I got caught in it. The Canadian Government could not take any responsibility for my boat or my life if I ignored this instruction, etc., etc.

It was beginning to look like the end of the line, for that year at least. Not only was it totally clear that I would not get through the Northwest Passage, I could not even reach an outpost of civilization such as Gjoa Haven, where Amundsen had wintered, or Cambridge Bay where there is a radar station. At either place I might have been able to lay the boat up safely for the winter and go home.

What if I could not make it back to Resolute? I already knew that ice was now pouring into Prince Regent Inlet, effectively slamming the back door on me. My concern was whether I could survive an arctic winter here. I had just about enough food and diesel oil but my clothing and sleeping bags were not really adequate for the winter temperatures which regularly drop to minus sixty degrees centigrade. The boat would be warmer but extremely cramped if I had to stick it out for several months of perpetual cold and darkness while the hut fell some way short of five-star accommodation.

And what about the polar bears? Inquisitive, immensely strong and deadly when hungry, they could easily smash their way into the hut if they felt that it contained their next meal. I did have an old .303 rifle but only about 30 rounds of ammo. which would soon disappear if I used it to shoot game.

While Captain Aye was away on his helicopter jaunt, I asked Tom Pullen where he thought I could anchor the boat so that she would not be dragged away by moving ice and we identified a small inlet on the chart which looked as if it would give reasonable shelter. I also asked if he thought *World Discoverer* would sell me some additional food and fuel as it was clear that I should stock up as much as possible against the possibility of having to spend the winter there.

When Captain Aye returned, he was in a great hurry to get under way and I found that the formerly cordial atmosphere was cooling somewhat. I think that, like the Coastguards, Captain Aye felt he might somehow be stuck with me and also I suppose he was feeling a little apprehensive about his own position. However Tom very decently asked him on my behalf about extra supplies and in a great hurry 75 gallons of diesel, a side of pork and 200 eggs were transferred to me in the ship's boat. I could see that Tom Pullen was very embarrassed by all this but as he was there simply as an adviser he could not press my case too hard.

After thanking Captain Aye for his hospitality and breakfast I returned to *Mabel* to take on board the supplies and was a bit shaken to receive a request for 400 Dollars. I said, truthfully, that I did not have that much cash on me and asked them to send me a bill which to their eternal credit they never did. I have a suspicion Tom Pullen talked them out of it. In any case, the diesel turned out to be waxy as it was not winter grade, the eggs all froze and burst and I never ate the pork!

In spite of this slight awkwardness, I was sorry, not to say a little worried, to see the *World Discoverer* disappear round the corner into Bellot Strait. I went for a walk ashore and began to take stock of my situation. The best bet would be to struggle back to Resolute but if this were not possible I must be prepared to stick it out at Fort Ross. The first thing would be to anchor the boat in a safe spot in shallow water so the big floes could not reach her. The small bay was within walking distance of the huts and looked reasonably promising.

Next, I decided that it would be better to take up residence ashore where there was more room than in *Mabel*'s cramped cabin. Assuming the heater could be made to work, I could transfer diesel from the boat to keep it running and I imagined I could pitch my tent inside the hut to give added protection from the cold. I would also transfer the cooker and

111

all sorts of stores from the boat. Using the dinghy I began ferrying some cans of fuel ashore with a view to getting the heater going. I thought I could board up the windows with planks salvaged from the other hut to make them more cold-proof and bear-proof. As it would be dark most of the time, it would not make any difference if the windows were glass or solid wood.

People at Resolute had told me how clever the polar bears were at stalking their prey, especially if they were hungry and so in order to have warning of a sneak attack, I surrounded the entrance of the hut with a ring of empty 45 gallon oil drums that were lying about the place. This burst of Boy Scout activity at least gave me a sense of purpose rather than just sitting around waiting for something to happen. The night-time temperature was between minus fifteen and minus twenty centigrade – colder than it ever becomes in England and new ice was forming on the sea. The prospect of a very long, lonely, uncomfortable period stretched ahead and made the idea of home and family seem more desirable than ever.

After 24 hours had passed, it seemed reasonable to assume that *World Discoverer* had made it through the strait and was now on her way through the rest of the Northwest Passage. Therefore it was a complete surprise when the ship suddenly reappeared after about 38 hours. It was early in the morning and I happened to walking along the foreshore at the time so I immediately leapt into the dinghy and rowed out to the boat so I could call the ship up on the VHF radio-telephone.

I spoke to an officer who said that Tom Pullen was asleep and that the ship was going straight on without stopping because they needed to get out of Prince Regent Inlet as fast as possible. Ice conditions were deteriorating and they might need further icebreaker assistance. They were not keen on the idea of my following them especially as they were not going back to Resolute. He revealed the incredible news that as she could not get through the Northwest Passage, *World Discoverer* would now extricate herself with all despatch, and sail at maximum speed for the Panama Canal which was her only alternative route to her next passenger pick-up at Tahiti. Resolute would be a major diversion in the wrong direction and anyway they could not waste time going at my speed.

It was not till later that I pieced together the full story. The ship had passed through the Bellot Strait but on emerging into Franklin Strait on the other side, had met total defeat at the hands of the ice. Not only had they failed to break through, they had found extraordinary difficulty in turning the ship round so as to return. With the icebreaker helping, it took nearly 12 hours to complete this manoeuvre! As the most experienced ice-pilot aboard, Tom Pullen had naturally been on the bridge throughout, which accounted for his being flat out asleep when I called the ship up. When he awoke and was told about my conversation, he came to my assistance once again by calling up the *Pierre Radisson* to report to them that I was still at Fort Ross.

Then it was 'goodbye' once again and with a boil of white water at her stern, the *World Discoverer* departed at top speed leaving me to my own devices. Peace then returned to Fort Ross. Two days later, however, a buzzing sound in the air announced the arrival of the Second in Command of the icebreaker who appeared in the ship's helicopter which settled in a swirl of dust near the huts. It really was very strange to be at one moment marooned in one of the most remote and desolate spots on the globe and at the next to have this little mechanical link with civilization drop out of the sky.

'What were my intentions?' he asked. I replied that if at all possible I would like to go back to Resolute so I could leave the boat there in safety for the winter. If the icebreaker was going to come out through Bellot Strait, it would be very nice if they could escort me. He said that he would have to obtain orders from Ottawa (as usual) and explained that his ship was standing by at the western exit of the strait in case they were needed to help a drilling barge that was trying to come up from Cambridge Bay. He then buzzed off again. One of the irritations was that because their vessel and mine were separated by high land, I could not contact them on VHF and, as already explained, I could not rely on the HF set which only worked when it felt like it.

Next day, the helicopter was back again with the same officer. What he had to say was not encouraging; the ice in Prince Regent Sound was now nine-tenths with new ice constantly forming. The *World Discoverer* had needed to call on the other icebreaker *Des Groseilliers* to help her escape into Lancaster Sound. It was becoming increasingly clear that *Mabel E.Holland* was not going anywhere, at least until next summer. The Coastguard officer outlined two possibilities. Either they would pick me up or they would let me have some additional supplies if I decided to stay put. After giving me this message, off he went again.

As expected, the barge could not get through due to ice conditions and after four days, *Pierre Radisson* was free to leave. Meanwhile I had spent my time finding the best possible anchorage for *Mabel E.Holland* and getting ready to leave at short notice, if need be. I found a pretty well-sheltered spot in shallow water where I hoped that she would not be affected by movements in the main body of pack-ice.

After the four days was up, the helicopter dropped out of the sky once again. This time the message was terse and to the point. The icebreaker would be coming through the strait in three hours time. Their bosses had said they could not escort *Mabel* to Resolute as it meant tying up the ship for several days for my exclusive benefit and might not succeed in any case. I had had plenty of time to think it over and immediately said I would accept a lift rather than stick it out at Fort Ross.

Under the circumstances it was obvious that discretion was the better part of valour.

Shortly afterwards the ship appeared and anchored. Meanwhile I had been galvanized into action and was very busy 'laying-up' *Mabel E.Holland*. I drained down the engine cooling systems so that frost would not crack them, poured Durogel into the fuel, which is supposed to stop it freezing, threw my clothes and papers into a kit-bag, disconnected the batteries and lifted them into the dinghy. I had anchored *Mabel* in the centre of the inlet and ran out warps to the shore so she would not be able to swing around. Having locked up the boat, I rowed ashore, deflated the dinghy and rolled it up and finally assembled everything in a neat little pile on the foreshore. The whole lot was loaded into the helicopter which to my slight surprise managed to lift it all into the air and drop us on the circular helipad on the stern of the icebreaker.

As we steamed around the headland and *Mabel E.Holland* was lost to view, I had to stand on deck with a lump in my throat and struggle with my private thoughts. When would I see her again – if ever?

Now that I was more-or-less off their conscience, everyone on the *Pierre Radisson* was very friendly. I saw that I would not have had the smallest chance of getting back to Resolute in *Mabel* and discovered that travelling aboard an icebreaker is not exactly a pleasure cruise. It took the best part of four days to reach Resolute and the grinding, shrieking, and crunching as the powerful ship smashed her way through the ice had to be heard to be believed. Restless is an understatement! They used to stop occasionally, just to give everyone a rest. When we reached Resolute, it was very different from when I had last seen it a month before. By mid-September the short summer was over and winter had set in. It was bitterly cold and the settlement was white with frost and snow. The sun had nearly gone, being no more than an orange blob on the horizon at midday.

An Esso tanker was unloading the winter fuel supply and on enquiry I was told that they would be pleased to take me on the pay-roll as a supernumerary spud-peeler. Having therefore arranged to leave the dinghy and batteries in a store and after many expressions of thanks to the captain and crew of *Pierre Radisson* I transferred to the tanker. In this manner I travelled in style if not in state as far as Halifax, Nova Scotia where I caught a plane to Boston and thence to London, arriving at the end of September. When I arrived at Heathrow, I was astonished to find that I had acquired some kind of minor notoriety, having been 'lost in the Arctic'. A representative of the *Daily Mail* offered to pay £750 for my story – I felt quite a celebrity!

Chapter 6

A hard grind

I RETURNED home feeling somewhat crestfallen. Not only had I failed to get through the North West Passage but I had also left the faithful *Mabel E.Holland* in a pretty perilous situation and furthermore returned much earlier than expected. Anyway, there was nothing to be done about it so I did my best to return to normality and picked up the threads of family and business life. Nevertheless, my thoughts were often with *Mabel* as I tried to imagine the storms, the perpetual darkness and the hellish cold of the arctic winter.

The 'sailing season' in the Arctic – in so far as it exists at all – is really confined to August and September and, finding it very difficult to contemplate leaving the boat unvisited for ten whole months, I decided to make an overland trip down to Fort Ross during May, 1987. This is traditionally the best time for sledge journeys: plenty of daylight, a chance of reasonable weather and yet the sea is still frozen solid. McClure, it will be recalled, became the first person to transit the North West

Passage when he and his crew walked from Banks Island to Melville Island having been stuck there for two years.

As this was just to be a reconnaissance, there was no reason to be single-handed and I was very pleased to be joined by my old friend Frederick Delouche, who thought that a trip to Fort Ross would be an opportunity not to be missed. So we took a flight from Heathrow to Edmonton and thence to Resolute where I was able to meet up with some of the people I had got to know the previous year and catch up with all the news. We placed ourselves in the hands of a firm called High Arctic International Explorers Ltd. run by Bezal Jesudason, who is an authority on polar exploration and advises and prepares the logistics for many professional expeditions to the North Pole. Bezal suggested that we take two Inuit guides, three skidoos and two sledges.

The skidoo is a cross between a sledge and a motor-bike having two steerable skiis at the front and a powerful 1000cc twin-cylinder bike engine driving a broad rubber belt with ridges on it at the back. You sit astride it like a bike and, if the terrain is flat and the load light, you can hurtle along at 60 mph leaving a plume of ice-crystals astern, like spray behind a speed-boat. For our expedition, however, our three skidoos were carrying a person each and towed two sledges carrying all our kit and fuel plus the fourth person and this cut the speed down to 20 mph at best or walking pace when negotiating broken ice. Even so, it was a whole lot easier than walking, let alone dragging a heavy sledge. I wondered what M'Clintock, who was regarded as the greatest sledging expert of his day, would have thought of these noisy but useful machines.

In contrast to the flashy modern outline of the skidoo, the sledges were strictly traditional, being approximately 3.4m (11ft) long and made of wood lashed together with rawhide thongs. This is because it is essential to let the sledge twist and bend as it goes over rough ice. If it could not 'work' in this way it would quickly break up under the strain.

118

The trip down to Fort Ross took three days of travelling nearly non-stop for around fourteen hours per day. On leaving Resolute, our route took us first across Barrow Strait, a 40-mile crossing leaving Griffith Island to starboard and heading towards Limestone Island, off the north-west point of Somerset Island. Limestone Island was easy to identify from its bold, bluff cliffs and after passing it we closed the shores of Somerset Island, passing Pressure Point and then on past Aston Bay and Cape Granite as we entered Peel Sound. We pressed on south along the shores of Somerset Island to about latitude 73 degrees north before turning inland towards the Stanwell-Fletcher Lake on our way across Somerset Island towards the settlement of Cresswell Bay. The temperature was between −15° and −20° Celsius so the seas and lakes were still frozen hard and the land still covered with snow.

While crossing the lake, we stopped to fish for Arctic Char which is similar to Salmon and excellent eating, with an average size of five or six pounds. The hard part was making a hole in the 4ft thick ice. Once this had been achieved, one could see the bottom clearly in about 12ft of water and a hand-line was dropped down bearing a hook and a silver-coloured metal lure. After a while the Char obligingly appeared and we were lucky enough to catch half a dozen in a short time, providing us with plenty of food for the next couple of days. It showed what an abundant place the Arctic is if you know where to look.

Cooking the fish was simple and carried out in the open. First the sledges would be positioned to create a windbreak and the Naphtha cookers would be lit under a pan full of snow which presently became boiling water. Meanwhile the fish were cleaned, cut into fillets, then boiled for a couple of minutes before being popped onto a plate with lashings of butter to provide a delicious and very sustaining meal.

The weather was good and with virtually constant daylight one only needs to stop to eat and rest. Our Inuit guides, short, stocky, dark-faced men seemed able to go on driving the skidoos for hour after hour while Frederick and I where soon aching in every limb from the bumping and jarring and deafened by the noise of the engines. Not exactly the most peaceful way of travelling. The compensation was the scenery: the towering mountains of Somerset Island and the spectacular pressure ridges in the ice on the west side of Prince Regent Inlet which soared up 9m (30ft) high or more above us. The idea of making this journey by water seemed an impossible dream. It was sunny the whole time we were travelling, with perfect visibility in the cold, dry air.

We tended to pitch camp at the warmest time of day and sleep for about six hours while most of the travelling was done at 'night- time' when the air temperature was cooler and the ice and snow crisper, so reducing the friction on the sledge runners.

Our next objective was Cresswell Bay where Bezal had arranged for us to pick up fuel. The skidoos are thirsty beasts, doing about eight miles to the gallon of petrol when pulling a sledge. This fuel had to be flown in by Twin Otter aircraft in 45-gallon drums and then transferred to the 5-gallon containers carried on the sledges. After a 10-hour stop at Cresswell Bay we set off again along the shores on the east side of Somerset Island, passing Cape Garry and following the coast more or less southwards before entering the area known as Hazard Inlet. This we crossed before heading on down toward Depot Bay where we hoped to find *Mabel*. The distance from Resolute, as the skidoo skiis, was just about 250 miles.

During this journey, I was on tenterhooks about what we should find at Fort Ross. There have been so many instances in the past of wooden vessels being crushed by moving ice that there was certainly no guarantee that *Mabel* would have survived the winter. The bay in which I had left her was small and horseshoe-shaped which I hoped would restrict any movement of ice through the narrow entrance.

When we reached Depot Bay, where I had anchored the boat nine months previously, to begin with there was no sign of her at all. It was quite difficult to find one's bearings as the scenery was so changed by being covered all over with white. Then I spotted a tell-tale flash of yellow and orange paint showing through what appeared to be a large mound of snow – she was completely buried. Recently-made polar bear footprints led up one side of this mound, right over the top of the coachroof and down the other side.

The first thing was to make camp so we skidoo'ed our way a further one-and-a-quarter miles to the Fort Ross huts where we unloaded our kit, cooked some food and slept for six hours. Then it was time to take a proper look at *Mabel*. She was frozen into the ice in an upright position which was a good start. The pressure of the ice had forced the bows up by about two feet but she was held firm at the aft end, probably due to the ice expanding in the propeller tunnels. This was a risk that I had not grasped when deciding to use the lifeboat for this voyage. A standard feature of traditional, heavy-displacement beach-launched lifeboats, the tunnels were useful in that they gave considerable protection to the props when working shallow waters but were also to prove something of an Achilles' heel for *Mabel*. Although I did not realize it at the time, expansion of the ice in these tunnels had placed an enormous stress on this area of the hull, and was most likely the cause of the hull continually leaking later on.

In preparing the boat I had some stainless steel sheeting fitted in the tunnel area abreast of the propellers because I thought that if the props struck ice they could smash it against the hull and possibly puncture a plank. However this did not really help to protect her from the effects of this terrific pressure caused by being solidly frozen in.

Blowing snow had drifted up against the hull and nearly succeeded in obliterating her completely. The first task, therefore was to set to work with shovels and clear the snow off to deck level so we could gain access to the hatches and the wheelhouse door. One of the precautions I had taken before leaving was to put plastic bags over the ventilators, secured with sticky tape, in an effort to keep out the snow but in the extreme cold the plastic had gone brittle and disintegrated in the wind. On opening the hatch of the forward compartment, which I use as the galley, I was most surprised to find it full of snow. The ventilators on *Mabel* do an excellent job of letting in air while keeping out water but the snow in the High Arctic is of a very fine, powdery texture and appears to have the ability to find its way through any crack or crevice. The idea of trying to live aboard the boat in the conditions that caused this hardly bore thinking about.

The aft cabin was in a better state with everything inside just as I had left it. With the wind moaning softly over the cabin-top, there was an eerie atmosphere on board due to the total lack of any movement. When a boat is afloat, even in fairly calm water, there is always some slight movement plus the sound of the water against the hull to give the impression that the vessel is alive. Solidly gripped by the arctic ice, *Mabel* was in a state of suspended animation. Above the chart table was the maximum and minimum thermometer which I noted had recorded a low of −58°C. The temperature at the time was a relatively bearable −15°C.

The next place to check was the engine-room and although the machinery was all glazed over with frozen condensation, it looked as it everything had survived extremely well. I had been prepared to find cracked castings and split pipework so it was a great relief to find that the sea-cocks and cooling-water pipes all appeared intact. Checking the bilges I could find no sign of any hull damage such as cracked frames and even some bottles of Grant's whisky were in one piece, unlike a bottle of Champagne which had shattered.

The lazarette, the small compartment in the stern above the propellers, was bone dry with no visible sign of damage. One of the characteristics of the arctic climate is very low humidity most of the time. So long as the temperature stayed below zero, everything was in effect 'freeze-dried' and there was none of the mould and mustiness that you would normally expect in a boat that had been sealed up for months. Working in these conditions brings on a terrible thirst but the cans of soft drink on board were useless to us being frozen solid and we had to melt snow to obtain any water.

The next job was to dig the snow out of the galley, which was handed up through the hatch in a bucket chain, and then to dig a trench around the hull so the sun could commence its work of melting the ice around the hull. This would otherwise have taken a lot longer as snow is a very good insulating material. We dug a trench about 5 feet wide right round the boat, down to ice level.

One of the most vulnerable features of the lifeboat was the rudder which sticks out beyond the stern. In RNLI usage it was designed to be raised for beaching but I had had it permanently fixed in the lowered position to reduce wear on the rudder-stock. I wanted to clear the rudder as much as possible and attach strong supporting lines because I feared that as the ice melted, it could exert heavy pressure on the rudder blade, in turn damaging the steering gear which had already been weakened the previous year. This little exercise occupied the four of us for nearly four hours using chisels, pickaxes and ordinary axes, as the ice was so astonishingly tough. In doing so I noticed that the heavy bronze steering quadrant support had cracked on the port side where water that had seeped in behind it had frozen. It is difficult to imagine the force that would be required to crack such a fitting, which in true RNLI style was about ten times stronger than required for normal service.

Curiously enough, it is important to strip off one's outer layers before any heavy physical work, even with the temperature well below zero, because if you perspire into your clothes, this will freeze later on. Some of the effects of the intense cold were quite bizarre. My plastic 'loo bucket, which I had left on deck, had simply split into about six pieces like a rotten banana.

We had now done about all we could to help *Mabel* survive the thaw and it was time to set off back to Resolute but before doing so I took the opportunity of asking my Inuit guides to show me how to make an igloo. First, we had to locate an area of compacted snow preferably .5-1m (2-3ft) deep in order to cut the snow blocks which would form the walls of the igloo. In cutting these blocks of, say .5-1m (2-3ft), a trench is formed which will be the entrance. The snow blocks are then placed in a circular fashion and with a snow knife angled off so that the next layer will automatically lean inwards to create the dome effect. The crevices between the blocks are grouted in with loose snow. The whole operation took about an hour and once completed gave total protection from the cold and wind. Inside the igloo, a bench is formed from further snow blocks and over this is draped a caribou hide before placing one's sleeping bag on top.

On our way back up the east shore of Somerset Island, we passed a couple of ancient Inuit settlements dating back a thousand years. One could clearly see the layout of the settlement and the size of the quarters as many of the whale bones that they used as the framing for huts were still intact. In due course we reached Cresswell Bay and once again filled our tanks with petrol for the second half of the journey.

Returning by the same route as on the outward journey, we had a near escape while crossing Barrow Strait when one of the skidoos nearly plunged into the sea through a crack that had appeared. After many hours of driving through the white-over scene, one's brain tended to slip into neutral but luckily one of the guides spotted the crack just in time. You cannot just stop abruptly or you will be struck smartly in the rear by a sledge weighing around half a ton so a quick turn is called for.

Of course, one must wear the very best kind of sunglasses all the time or the constant glare of sun on snow will quickly lead to snow-blindness. Many of the early European explorers suffered disastrously from snow-blindness and apparently failed to notice the wooden discs or pieces of bone with narrow slits in them that the Inuit placed over their eyes to cut down the brightness.

This early reconnaissance lasted a fortnight and on the whole I was very encouraged by the state in which I had found *Mabel* and was quietly confident that there was a good chance of us getting through the North West Passage that year. My plan was to return in the first week of August and be ready to move two weeks later. If only I knew just how over-optimistic these plans were!

On my return to England, I was able to continue with a programme of up-grading my equipment as it had been clear that I was not properly prepared to winter in the Arctic, should that become necessary. The most important items were a much superior tent from Ultimate and two heavy-duty sleeping bags reputed to keep one warm in a temperature of −40°! There was also a new Browning rifle to replace the ancient .303 and a back-up portable radio from Plessey.

This orderly plan of campaign was thrown to the winds after I received a phone call from Canada, late one evening near the end of July. It was Bezal Jesudason saying that he had just received a report from the crew of the Canadian Ice Patrol aircraft who had spotted *Mabel E.Holland* apparently lying awash on the foreshore. Apparently the ice in Depot Bay had broken up following a severe storm and it looked as if *Mabel* had been flooded and pushed ashore. This was an appalling shock and I could only mutter my thanks for the information and say I would make my way to Resolute at the first opportunity.

This proved easier said than done as all flights to Edmonton and on to Resolute were fully booked and I had to go on a waiting list just to reach Canada. Once in Edmonton my problems were far from over as the twice-weekly flight to Resolute is always half-filled with cargo and had a lengthy waiting list for passengers. However, after 24 hours at Edmonton I managed to get on a flight which left late in the evening as it was becoming dark, but as we passed the Arctic Circle, it gradually became lighter again until we arrived in twilight at about 3am. It was mid-summer in Edmonton but in Resolute the thermometer stood at zero degrees Celsius and it was snowing.

I remembered that when we had flown up in May, looking out of the window had been like looking at a blank sheet of paper but now the outlook was totally different. The tundra was clear of snow and there were pools of water everywhere, prevented from soaking away by the permafrost below. There are no trees but when flying over the sea, one could now see the various islands, straits and inlets and it was interesting to see the ice beginning to break up and be carried along by the wind. The blue seawater made a striking contrast with the white pack-ice and looked almost inviting.

In reality, conditions were particularly bleak when I arrived at Resolute on 6th August and there was no chance of continuing down to Fort Ross for the time being. The only way to reach there would be to charter a Twin Otter aircraft. These remarkable flying workhorses can carry up to twenty people or two tons of freight and can land and take off from very short and rough strips. As can be imagined, chartering one is not cheap but I found that I could share a charter with

126

some scientists who were at Fort Ross and waiting to come back to Resolute.

I had arranged to stay with Buster Welsh who I had met the previous year and who runs the research department of Canadian Fisheries at Resolute. Due to my enforced idleness I was able to look up some other friends including Pat Gaulton who worked for Canadian Transport at the airport. Pat had very kindly been looking after *Mabel*'s batteries and Tinker Traveller dinghy and these were now brought out and checked, ready for loading onto the aircraft.

There are no facilities for aircraft whatever at Fort Ross other than a reasonably flat and boulder-free piece of ground so it was pointless to take off from Resolute without being pretty confident that the weather was clear 250 miles away. The crew of two appeared extremely laid back and casual but were in fact totally professional as flying in the Arctic is not something to be undertaken lightly.

Larry Solar, the Ice Patrol Officer who I met the previous year, was at Resolute and he told me that he had a piece of video of *Mabel* taken at the time she had been spotted from the air. This turned out to be pretty disappointing as the boat could only be seen as a vague blob on the screen for a few seconds and you certainly could not tell anything about her condition.

The bad weather continued for the next five days and I took the opportunity to obtain some additional kit such as boots, mukluks, waders, caribou gloves plus two 'come-alongs'; tackles which could be useful for dragging the boat off the shore. Finally the plane was able to leave on the morning of August 10th. During the hour-and-a-half flight I was able to have a close look at the ice conditions. Lancaster Sound was fairly clear but Peel Sound appeared solid, in spite of the north-east wind. We flew at less than a thousand feet giving a clear view of the ground as we crossed Somerset Island. Without its snow covering the land is a rather featureless reddish-brown colour and the terrain one of mountains, valleys and ravines with pools of water lying in any hollow spot.

After flying for an hour and a half we arrived over Fort Ross and the pilot, Duncan, circled to find a landing spot as close to the boat as possible and after touching down he kindly taxied the plane as close to the shore as he could to save me having to hump all my heavy gear. He then picked up the two scientists and their stuff and after about 45 minutes on the ground was away, leaving me to my own devices.

I had spotted the boat from the air, looking extremely forlorn with the water lapping over her decks but it was not until the sound of the departing aircraft faded into the distance that the complete silence and the bleakness of the surroundings began to weigh on me. As I got to work transferring my gear to the waterside, sleet was starting to fall.

The first task was to pump up the dinghy and load my gear into it. I rowed about a quarter of a mile across the bay to the boat and when I reached her, lying heavily in the water, I seriously wondered if this was to be the journey's end. It was a deeply depressing sight and it took a lot of mental effort to galvanize myself into some kind of useful action.

The first thing was to pitch the tent on the foreshore so I could keep some of the gear dry. I then went back to the boat and climbed on board. On opening the wheelhouse door, I was greeted by the sight of water everywhere with bits of food and waterlogged clothing floating in an oily scum. The main food store under the floorboards was completely submerged. I then went forward to the engine-room to find the water covering the gearboxes and halfway up the engines themselves. How would I ever manage to get them running, I wondered? The forward compartment was totally flooded as well, with all sorts of gear and food sloshing around in oily water. It then being about 8pm I thought it would be best to make a meal and snatch some sleep, ready for an early start next day.

In the morning I set up the Plessey radio in the tent and called up Buster Welsh who had arranged to listen for me at 0800, 1200 and 1800 each day. I told him I thought it was all over and that I would have to write the boat off but he was very supportive and urged me not to give up and in the end I said I would stick with it at least till I could find out what had caused the boat to sink.

I spent the whole of that day pumping and bailing out icy seawater. A boat that has been flooded is the most depressing thing imaginable, the normally orderly interior being a total chaos of soaking clothing, ruined food and bits of soggy paper all sloshing around in oily water. To add to the fun it sleeted hard all day and all that night. By the time I staggered ashore to the tent at about 11pm, all my clothes were soaking wet and I was shivering with cold but oddly enough I did not feel quite so depressed as I felt that the day's labour had actually achieved something.

Another day of pumping got the water-level down sufficiently to reveal the sea-cocks. I felt sure I was going to find a cracked pipe with water spurting in and, of course, this would have been relatively simple to fix but nothing of the kind appeared. Instead, I realized that water was steadily seeping into the lazarette from the propeller tunnels on both sides. The boat was gradually coming upright but at this stage I had no idea if she could be made seaworthy so I began taking off some of the equipment and removing spoiled food for disposal ashore.

At low tide I was able to examine the underside of the hull. A rope had wrapped itself round the port propeller with the result that the castle-nut that holds it on had stripped its thread. Apart from this, there was no visible damage. In one way this was encouraging because it made me feel the boat could be made seaworthy but at the same time it was worrying because I could not see how the water was finding a way in. Due to the 'double-diagonal' construction, with two layers of planking laid at an angle, it is possible for water to gain access in one place and travel a considerable distance between the skins before emerging somewhere totally different.

That evening at about 10.30 I saw a polar bear stroll past my tent and I thought it prudent to spend the night on the boat, in spite of the cold and damp. The sleet continued to fall.

Once the engine-room was free of water, I could think about trying to get the engines running. First I drained contaminated oil from the gearboxes and replaced it with fresh. The lubricant in the main engine sumps appeared to be unaffected. Using the hand starting gear, I turned the engines over in the hope of getting some oil to the various moving parts which must have been dry following the long period of idleness. Next, I ferried the main batteries on board and charged them up using a small Honda generator that I had brought down with me on the aircraft. This was proving an absolutely gem as I had it running on deck every day and without it the batteries would have been flat in no time and there would have been no hope of starting the diesels. Meanwhile the Gardners would turn over, but showed absolutely no signs of firing.

Once the boat was properly afloat again, I transferred the radio to its normal position aboard and got a better signal from the tall whip aerial than from the piece of wire I had rigged up in the tent. Each day, I called up Buster Welsh to report the situation and he in turn made helpful suggestions. He was a great morale booster and when I reported that I could not obtain the slightest sign of life from the engines he said he was sure I would succeed eventually. The radio was a real lifeline and made one ponder on the incredible mental stress that the old explorers must have felt after being totally cut off from civilization for years on end.

After several days had passed Buster came up with a brilliant idea. He told me that the Twin Otter was going to make a supply trip to Cresswell Bay, about 100 miles north on Somerset Island and suggested I might do a deal, offering them some of my fuel in return for the plane continuing to Fort Ross with supplies I needed. This was actually quite a good arrangement for the settlement as all their fuel had to be flown in while *Mabel* was virtually fully loaded with about 950 gallons of diesel – far more than I needed either to motor back to Resolute or on to Cambridge Bay, should that prove possible. In return I would be able to get hold of a new heating stove to replace one made inoperable by submersion, an additional heavy-duty battery, a submersible electric pump plus a second Honda to run it and 15 gallons of petrol. Perhaps the most important items were some spray cans of ether to squirt into the engine air-intakes when attempting to start them. This is a well-known trick for encouraging reluc-tant diesels as it gets the engine turning even before the fuel is coming through properly.

Amazingly, there was no objection to carrying all this fuel, batteries, chargers etc. on the aircraft in contrast to commercial airlines which ban anything flammable. The Twin Otter could apparently carry 46 of my 5-gallon plastic con-tainers and when I spoke to Buster at 0800 on the 15th he told me the plane would arrive at 1300 the same day so I imme-diately went into top gear lugging the cans over to the airstrip. The long-suffering Tinker Traveller dinghy could carry ten cans and I would row as close to the strip as possible before unloading and carrying the cans the rest of the way, each round trip taking an hour and ten minutes. The quarter-mile walk was tiring as the surface, although reasonably flat was either loose shale and boulders or soggy peat. The aircraft landed while I was on my fourth trip.

Buster had entrusted my supplies to a person called Aussie – or perhaps it was Ossie as there was nothing

Australian about him – who was flying down to Cresswell Bay to visit his in-laws. I persuaded him to come and help me try to start the engines by hand – something that is virtually impossible to do single-handed. As before, they refused to fire and Aussie, who rather prided himself on his mechanical knowledge – gave the opinion that they would need to be stripped down and the pumps and injectors checked. We walked back to the aircraft to find that the ever-helpful crew had already loaded up the cans and were ready to go. I thanked them profusely and watched while the sturdy machine bounced and wallowed over the rough ground before staggering into the air with its heavy load of diesel fuel.

Alone once again, I ferried the new supplies back to the boat and was quite surprised to find it was already 6pm. How time flies when you're having fun!

Just as on a long single-handed passage, I found it was important to stick to a daily routine and I used to start preparing my main meal of the day at about 8pm. There was not a great deal of variety as my food consisted of prepared, vacuum-packed meals which only needed to be heated up in a pan of boiling water. Of course there were different packs to choose from such as curry, coq au vin, lasagna and so on. Pudding invariably consisted of a tin of fruit. I was interested to find that raspberries and plums had survived being frozen without any apparent deterioration whereas peaches, pineapples and other fruits were less appetizing as they tended to break down into a mush. Coffee or tea rounded off the meal. I had also brought out a large supply of peanuts which I could ration out and nibble during the day.

Next morning the sun was shining brightly and in view of the previous day's heavy programme, I decided to take the day off for a little exploring. The temperature during August varied from about −5° to +6° C with most days averaging 2-3 degrees above freezing. In the sunshine, it was really very pleasant and I set off to climb the hill overlooking Depot Bay, on the top of which was the remains of a cairn supporting a flagstaff.

From the top I could look down over Port Kennedy where M'Clintock and the crew of the steam-yacht *Fox* had wintered in 1858 while trying to establish the fate of the Franklin expedition. In those days they had been totally on their own devices, with no radio, position finding equipment, no proper charts, very little heating and no entertainment other than what they made for themselves. They had to survive temperatures down to −60° C and more or less continuous darkness from November to February. In spite of this, a number of outstanding sledge journey were mounted from *Fox* which resulted in the Franklin mystery being finally cleared up. During *Fox*'s stay at Port Kennedy, only two men died and the vessel was successfully extricated the following year and returned to England.

The scenery is amazing with a great deal of contrast and there always seemed to be animals in sight – caribou, foxes, lemmings and arctic hares – while flights of Brent Geese would occasionally pass overhead. With no other human within a hundred miles, it was the most peaceful and serene place I had ever known.

Refreshed from this day off, I returned to the job of trying to get the engines going with new energy and resolve. Since the visit of the Twin Otter, I had left the new heater burning in the engine-room in the hope of warming and drying the machinery. By sheer luck I decided to concentrate on the starboard engine which turned out to be the better prospect. Draining out the lubricating oil, I heated it up in a metal can before pouring it back into the engine which thereafter turned over more easily but still would not start. After turning it over by hand a few times, I positioned myself with one hand holding an ether spray-can in front of the air-intake and the other on the electric starter button. Twice the engine spluttered and banged as it sucked in the ether but died as soon as I took my finger off the button but the third time, to my intense relief, it caught and fired, at first horribly roughly but gradually smoothing down as each cylinder warmed up and settled into its accustomed steady rhythm. This was on the 21st of August, 11 days after I had arrived and was the real turning point in my battle to save the boat and the whole project. Even with just one Gardner ticking over, gradually warming up its mass of cold metal, pumping water steadily through the cooling system and drying out the generator, the totally lifeless feel had been banished from the boat and there seemed to be a glimmer of hope.

I then turned my attention to the port engine but in spite of following the same procedure, there was no response. There did not seem to be much compression so I took out an injector and inserted a length of plastic tubing through the hole into the cylinder. Sucking on this, I was dismayed to find a mixture of dirty water and emulsified diesel coming up. It then hit me that the fuel in the port-side main tank must have been contaminated with sea-water when it was submerged. To test this theory I disconnected the fuel supply and dropped the intake pipe into one of the plastic cans of fuel. Then I carefully sucked out each cylinder in turn and dribbled in some oil to help the compression. Finally, I flushed the whole fuel system through and changed the filters and eventually this engine also grumbled reluctantly into life.

Now that I knew where the problem lay with the fuel, it was a relatively simple matter to drain the 50-gallon port main tank and take the contaminated fuel ashore before replacing it with fresh diesel from cans. After everything was properly warmed up I changed the gearbox oil a second time. Once all this had been done and the whole engine-room had been tidied up with everything back in its proper place, I was able to transfer my attention to the damaged castle nut which retains the seals on the port outer shaft bearing.

To do this, it was necessary to drag *Mabel* as far inshore as possible at high tide in the hope that the shaft would be exposed as the water retreated. However, even wearing the chest-high waders that I had thoughtfully obtained in Resolute, this turned out to be an extremely wet and awkward job. Due to the very limited clearance under the hull I was forced to crouch or virtually lie down to get at the offending part and this allowed the water to trickle agonizingly over the top of the waders. Nevertheless, I cut away the tangled rope from the shaft, screwed back the castle nut as far as its damaged thread would allow and secured it with Monel seizing wire. I felt there was a good chance this would hold if I went easy with the revs on that side.

Next time I spoke to Buster, I had the great satisfaction of being able to report that *Mabel* and I were back in business, the only problem being that Depot Bay was once more full of ice so we could not actually go anywhere. As M'Clintock found, one of the advantages of Fort Ross is convenient high land from which the Bellot Strait could be overlooked. From time to time I would scramble up to the peak for a look-see but the result was never very encouraging. The strait was completely full of ice and it was looking as if conditions generally were as bad, or even worse, than the previous year. The ice reports that were relayed to me indicated that Peel Sound, Franklin Strait and James Ross Strait remained unbroken and as it was now nearly the end of August, only a few more melt days could be expected. That left me with two possibilities: motoring back to Resolute or beaching *Mabel* at Fort Ross. The former was clearly more attractive as it would be far easier to work on repairs at Resolute. From this year's disaster it was obvious the boat could not be left afloat and needed to be got ashore if she was to survive at all. Buster concurred and said there was a good chance of a lead opening up on the east side of Somerset Island, which would give me a fighting chance of retreating to Resolute.

Before leaving England, I had had correspondence with an American named John Bockstoce, a nephew of President George Bush, who is a yachtsman and an Arctic enthusiast. He had devoted an enormous amount of effort trying to get through the North West Passage from the Pacific side, in his large and capable 18.9m (62ft) steel motor-sailer *Belvedere*. He had rounded Cape Barrow and managed to reach a settlement called Tuktoyaktuk, just east of Herschel Island but had been obliged to leave the boat there for the next two years due to the severe ice conditions. This year he was hoping to 'break out' into Lancaster Sound.

In his letter, John had given me various radio frequencies and times when he would keep a listening watch in the hope that I would be able to make contact. I also had the telephone number of a friend of his named Peter Semotiuk who lived at Cambridge Bay and was in daily contact with John. With more time to spare I therefore spoke to Buster Welsh on the radio who in turn telephoned Peter Semotiuk (they have direct-dial phones in the High Arctic, naturally!) and he in turn alerted John Bockstoce to the fact that I was 'on the air'. By this means, contact was established and I had the great boost of being able to exchange news daily. When I first spoke to John, *Belvedere* had made considerable progress and was close to Cambridge Bay where there is a Distant Early Warning radar station (part of the so-called DEW-line) and consequently an air-strip. However the ice reports were not at all encouraging and it seemed quite possible that he would have to back-track to Tuktoyaktuk once again.

In this part of the world one has to be an optimist as it is quite common for a stretch of water that is totally impassable one day to offer a passage the next. Time and time again I have heard it said that patience is the key when navigating in ice, as openings can appear when you are least expecting them to.

Bockstoce is a man who does things in style! On the 25th August he told me he was hoping to charter a single-engine ski-plane based at Cambridge Bay that would be able to land on the ice near the yacht and then take him on a personal ice patrol of the area. Even so I had no idea he planned to fly over to Fort Ross so when I heard the sound of an aircraft I assumed it to be the Canadian Ice Patrol and when I called up on VHF Channel 16 I was amazed to hear the voice of John Bockstoce in reply. He said he was not over-optimistic about making further progress that year but mentioned the possibility of our meeting at the western exit of Bellot and then travelling up Peel Sound in company to Resolute. Whether this proved possible remained to be seen but in the mean time it was a great fillip to one's morale being in contact with John.

Next day I continued with the task of collecting various items from the landing strip but overnight ice began drifting into the bay which made it impossible to use the dinghy. Later the wind increased to 30 knots from the south-west with light snow but this was a hopeful sign as it could push the ice off the eastern shore of Somerset Island. In the late evening I climbed up to my usual lookout point: Bellot Strait was still blocked but looking north across Hazard Inlet it looked as if the ice had been pushed about two miles away from the shore.

The strong wind kept up for the next two days and kept pushing ice into the bay until I could not use the dinghy at all. Fetching items from the airstrip therefore became very hard work as each day I walked about 40 miles to and fro, carrying loads of 60-70 pounds. At least I was keeping fit! I also took the opportunity to fill four cans with fresh water from a nearby lake.

The time had come for me to make my attempt at a break-out. By the 27th, there was a definite feel of winter in the air and I was well aware that time was running short. *Belvedere* forced her way through to Gjoa Haven on this day but could make no further progress. Finally, on the 30th I

137

decided to 'go for it' and was up and ready to leave by 0300, the time of high water. There was a lot of ice in Depot Bay and after recovering the anchors, I had to crash and shove a way through to find a way out of the bay. At least there was the reassurance of hearing the Gardners come up to full power and a great relief when nothing broke or fell off. Having got clear, I anchored again near the Fort Ross huts and rowed ashore so as to climb the look-out hill. The view to the northward looked reasonably hopeful with black streaks among the white so it was quickly back on board to get under way.

The first problem was to cross Bellot Strait as ice was now pouring out of it on the current. My idea was to take up station behind a large floe and follow it as it crashed its way through smaller pieces. After some very tricky moments when the boat was stuck between floes, we managed to cross into relatively clear water. Afterwards things went reasonably well to begin with; I managed to round first Long Island and then Brown Island and make about 10 miles of headway to the north. But that was it. A solid barrier of 8/10ths density pack-ice made further progress impossible and there was still something like 140 miles to go to Prince Leopold Island. There was nothing for it but to turn back which I did with a heavy heart. Just returning to Depot Bay was a major problem as re-crossing Bellot Strait was even more difficult than before and poor *Mabel* had to endure some severe knocks and nips from the ice. To get back into Depot Bay I had to wait for high water and then creep along the shore with the boat bumping over the bottom in order to pass inside the heavy ice grounded further out. Eventually, by late afternoon, we were back in the old familiar spot with anchors down and lines to the shore.

My guardian angel must have been working overtime that day as very shortly after mooring the boat securely, the wind swung to the south-east and began to blow very hard, bringing snow and an abrupt fall in temperature. Within an hour, it was screaming at over 50 knots with horizontal snow reducing visibility to virtually nil. Had I been caught out in Prince Regent Inlet on a lee shore with the ice driving in on the gale, I should have been in very serious difficulties. At 2200 I managed to contact *Belvedere* and found that they too were having their work cut out coping with drifting ice and dragging anchors at Spence Bay. The barometer fell 30 millibars in five hours.

In the morning my sleeping bag was covered with snow that had blown in through a tiny gap I left open for ventilation. Outside, everything was white, the bay was full of ice and the dinghy was swamped. Lying shivering in my bunk I faced up to the fact that I was not going anywhere in 1987 and that the only thing to do was make plans to somehow haul the boat out of the water. I felt this was essential because she was leaking heavily and needed pumping out every day. My fear was that if she went through the freezing process in this condition, water would freeze between the layers of planking and open it up even more.

The first thing was to look for a place where it might be possible to drag the boat above high water mark. Although Depot Bay provided a secure anchorage, its shores are mostly fairly steep and boulder-strewn but eventually I managed to find a place on the western side where the beach sloped gently and was predominantly sand and gravel. There was about 30 yards of beach above the high water mark, terminating in a low cliff which could serve as the anchorage point for a hauling system of some kind. There were three big boulders obstructing the ideal hauling-out spot but after moving the boat to this new location I managed to shift them using *Mabel*'s capstan and a tackle anchored to the cliff.

I also gave thought as to how I might relaunch the boat having once beached her. The anchors, though substantial, would not have the holding power to shift a weight of 20 tons but very fortunately I spotted a massive boulder lying in about 1.2m (4ft) of water, some 77m (85 yards) offshore. I reckoned that when the time came I could drop a loop of steel cable over this rock and haul the boat out to it.

The morning after the storm, I managed to speak first to *Belvedere* and later to Buster Welsh at our two scheduled times. John Bockstoce said he had decided to abandon his efforts for the time being and backtrack to Tuktoyaktuk where there was equipment capable of hauling *Belvedere*'s 39-tons out of the water.

Buster Welsh told me that the wind had been recorded at 75 knots in Resolute and that everyone had been confined indoors. He also reminded me that he and his organization would be flying out of Resolute on 1st September as their season's stint was complete. This would be a real blow as he had been such a tremendous support during the whole of August, not only in having equipment rounded up and sent down to me but in constantly encouraging me to keep up the fight to get the boat afloat and in working order. Even as he prepared to leave, he was arranging to borrow a power winch and the other material I needed to drag the boat out of the water. Not having him on the other end of the radio was a loss I would feel very keenly.

Caribou were starting to appear in increasing numbers as they began their autumn migration. Even during the gale a group of four had been feeding along the shores of the bay, keeping company with a family of snow geese but at dusk on the 1st September, a group of 40 of these big, handsome animals wandered slowly past the boat. Even this was only the advance party for a couple of days later nearly 300 Caribou made their way slowly by, taking around four hours to do so. They were working their way round the bay and heading in a northerly direction towards the areas where they would spend the winter foraging for moss and lichen under the snow. Their coats looked superb, as indeed they needed to be to protect them from the hostile environment through the long winter. I also saw an Arctic Fox and noticed that its coat was in the process of changing from its summer browny-red to winter white.

Wildlife of another kind gave me a tremendous shock a couple of days later when I was working on one of the propellers at low tide. I glanced up from this job to find a polar bear not more than 3.5 metres (12 ft) away. I am not sure which of us had the biggest fright but at least he (or she) was surprised enough to stand still while I clambered rather smartly back on board. Calming down a bit, I grabbed my camera and began taking photographs from quite close range. After a while, the bear came right up to the boat and stood on its hind legs with front paws resting on the rubber fender and huge face peering through the lifelines. Thinking that this was quite close enough I shouted in what I hoped was a threatening manner bringing a snarl in reply. As its paws slipped down the fender, the claws gouged out marks that left no doubt as to their sharpness.

Next, the bear decided to investigate the various items of equipment lying around on the foreshore, beginning by sniffing carefully at some cans of diesel. I knew these animals were tremendously strong but confess to being quite startled to see this one pick up a 32kg (70lb) kitbag in its teeth and shake it casually like a dog playing with a stick. The next item to come under scrutiny was the inflatable dinghy. I did not object to him sniffing at it, or even bouncing up and down on it but had to take exception when he started to bite the rubber as this was a piece of equipment I could not do without. I already had the rifle at hand and now fired a warning shot which had the desired effect as he left the dinghy and shambled off in the direction of the cabins.

He kept me under surveillance for some time afterwards and even returned to the boat when I was away on an errand but fortunately made no move to prevent me getting back on board. Eventually he departed and I wondered whether he was in fact a she looking for a suitable den. Imagine if I had returned the next year to find a family of bear cubs gambolling around the decks!

After prevaricating for a few more days in the hope of a last-minute favourable change in the weather, or the providential arrival of an ice-breaker, I took the decision to go ahead with my scheme for a winter lay-up on the spot. Buster Welsh having by then departed, I called up Bezal and Terry Jesudason and asked them to continue rounding up the equipment I had asked for and to book the Twin Otter to bring the stuff down with some volunteer helpers. Meanwhile, I got on with preparing the boat. I still had plenty of fuel cans and in order to lighten the boat I transferred most of the fuel from the main tanks into 80 of them, which thereafter made a slightly bizarre sight lined up in the snow.

I then beached the boat at high tide and at low water removed a blanking-off plug in the keel that covered the large aperture that had been used to attach hauling tackles in her lifeboat days. At least the boat was designed for hauling over the beach. In addition to the enormously strong attachment point in the keel, she has bilge runners to protect the hull and stop her from falling on her side. She could in fact be dragged over pretty rough terrain without damage, if a powerful enough winch was available.

And that turned out to be the problem. When my 'rescue party' finally flew in on Monday 7th September, they turned out to be a motley crew with a heap of inappropriate and untested equipment. One winch which had been flown all the way from Resolute at my expense proved to have stripped gears making it totally useless and that really set the tone for the whole ghastly day.

As soon as the plane taxied to a stop, the door opened and an Inuit stood in the doorway with a rifle and shot a caribou. I was most offended as the animals had become like friends and most probably had become accustomed to my presence. Of course the Inuit look on these animals as food in the same way as we regard cattle. Six people jumped down from the door, including the pilot and navigator and two of the Inuit went off to examine their kill while the others began unloading the equipment.

Having been assured on the radio that all the stuff had been checked, I felt a sinking feeling as soon as I saw the Honda trike and trailer that were vital parts of the whole exercise as it was immediately apparent that the tow hitch was broken. In spite of efforts to lash the trike and trailer together it was obvious that it would not survive carrying heavy loads over rough ground for very long. The first job for the trailer was to carry the caribou carcass to the plane, so getting everything well covered in blood.

As for the equipment that was being brought out of the plane, I could see at a glance that it would not be man enough to pull a 20-ton boat up a slope. The winches were the kind usually fitted to the back of Caterpillar crawlers and were clearly marked 2.5 tons but the significance of the little dot between the 2 and 5 did not appear to have got through to the people at Resolute who were under the impression that they had a pulling power of 25 tons. And as already mentioned, one winch had a broken reduction gear, making it virtually useless.

I began to realize that I was sponsoring a day out for the boys rather than a serious effort to shift my boat but figuring that every volunteer is worth seven pressed men, I bit my lip and consoled myself with the thought that miracles do occasionally happen. The Inuit were put in charge of transporting the equipment to the boat as they seemed to have an affinity with partly-destroyed Honda trikes and after much persistence and four round trips the majority of the winching equipment, wood, wire hawsers, come-alongs etc. were deposited at the boat.

The first objective was to use a hydraulic jack to raise the bow in order to insert greased timbers under the keel. However the ground was too soft and there was nothing strong enough to stand the jack on so it just drove itself down into the mud. We continued trying to lift the bow, using timbers and rocks as levers but it was hopeless trying to raise a weight of 20 tons in this way.

We therefore dug a small trench just in front of the boat and placed a sleeper in it for the keel to slide over. Then we connected all the winching gear up, fixing one end to the rockface with crow-bars and the other to the hauling-point on the lifeboat's keel. When everything was as ready as it could be, I went on board and started one of the engines so that I could use the ship's own powered capstan to heave on a further hawser to the rocks. When the strain was applied, *Mabel* refused to move so much as a fraction of an inch. After a few repeated attempts at heaving, shoving, pulling and levering it was obvious that we were wasting our time and there was nothing to be done but pack up the whole motley collection and haul it all back to the plane.

The fun of this outing was by now definitely starting to pall as the trailer had disintegrated and the trike was playing up, so much of the equipment had to be manhandled over about two miles of roughish terrain. I had intended to return on the plane to Resolute and I therefore took off *Mabel*'s four heavy-duty batteries, weighing 40kg (90lbs) each, which I put into the dinghy so as to row them across the bay nearer to the aircraft. Ice obstructed my usual landing-place so I had a longish walk carrying each of these batteries in turn. It was lucky that after a month of hard physical work each day I was fairly fit as otherwise I would have been totally exhausted by this task alone.

Before the saga could finally close, the 80 cans of fuel which I had laboriously taken ashore had to be put back on board again, and while stowing these below I slipped down the forward hatch, badly pulling a muscle in my arm. Eventually all the stuff including the dinghy was loaded onto the aircraft and topped off with three dead caribou. It was not until 10.30 in the evening that we finally took off, in darkness, for the flight to Resolute. All of us except the pilot and navigator just collapsed in exhaustion and I take my hat off to those two, who had worked as hard as anyone in ferrying the equipment.

On landing at Resolute it was snowing hard and bitterly cold and I could not have been more delighted to jump into a warm utility wagon and go to Bezal and Terry Jesudason's place where they were waiting with a hot meal and, wonder of wonders, a hot bath. After a month of distinctly spartan living I looked and felt pretty dishevelled and the sensation of lying between clean sheets in a comfortable bed in a warm cabin was almost unreal.

When we had reached Resolute in the middle of the night, we just staggered off the aircraft and left everything as it was so the first task next day was to unload everything and sort it out. Most of the hauling equipment came back to Bezal and Terry's while the dinghy and batteries were taken to Pat Gaulton at the Transport Depot who had looked after them before and kindly offered to do so again.

The weather was miserable – cold and foggy – so I made the best of it by visiting friends in Resolute. By happy coincidence I was able to meet Jo and Jeff MacInnis, father and son, who are well-known in Canada for having led a diving expedition on *HMS Breadalbane*, a supply ship involved in the search for Franklin, which had been crushed by ice and sunk off Cape Riley in 1853. In addition, Jo had dived with Prince Charles at the North Pole. They were at Resolute because Jeff and Mike Beedell were engaged in attempting to sail from Tuktoyaktuk to Pond Inlet in a Hobiecat. They started out during 1986 and finally reached their objective two years later. In 1987 they managed to progress from

Cambridge Bay to Cape Ann, more or less opposite Resolute on the other side of Lancaster Sound in spite of the exceptionally bad ice conditions. The advantage of their seemingly inappropriate craft was that it could sail in very shallow water and that, if the worst came to the worst they could actually drag it over the ice. Although I admired their efforts, it is worth pointing out that they did not cover anything like the whole Northwest Passage, which is defined as being from Davis Strait to Bering Strait. In some publications they are credited with 'sailing through the Northwest Passage' which is overstating the case considerably.

One visit which was to prove exceptionally useful was to Tao and Link Washburn, who invited me to dinner one evening. They shared my disappointment at the season's lack of progress and felt as much concern as I did about leaving the boat at Fort Ross in its present condition. One suggestion they made was that I contact an outfit called Narwhal Arctic Services who were involved in moving heavy equipment around, generally for the oil industry.

Next day, therefore, I went to their base and explained my problem to one of the partners, named Gordy. He agreed that my scheme for hauling the boat out should be perfectly feasible but pointed out that the real difficulty lay in finding sufficiently powerful winches that were light enough to be air-portable. The trick was to make up a complete kit of equipment which would not exceed the maximum weight that the Twin Otter could carry in addition to the people we would need. He promised to look into the problem and give me an answer as soon as possible.

After a couple of days Gordy told me he had identified a type of compact 24-volt electric winch designed for fitting to heavy overland trucks, which had a pulling power of 12,000 lbs (5,500kg). These could be obtained off the shelf in Edmonton and sent up by air. Gordy calculated that two of these winches, pulling via a 6:1 purchase, would give the power we needed. A slight drawback was the fact that they cost $2,000 each, plus air-freight and that the cost of chartering the Twin Otter for a further day would be $2,500. The cost of the whole operation was frightening but feeling I had little choice, I took a deep breath and agreed. I hoped to soften the blow somewhat by selling the winches when I had finished with them and by borrowing some of the basic items such as wire rope.

The Narwhal people immediately set to work, not only assembling gear but to my delight laying it out and testing it. After the new winches arrived they set them up on a pair of huge Caterpillar crawlers with the other ends of the tackles attached to three more of these mechanical monsters. This outfit succeeded in dragging the first pair of crawlers bodily across the ground without anything breaking, which seemed to me a most impressive demonstration.

A list of all the items we would need was carefully prepared as follows:

Honda trike and trailer (not broken)
2 heavy-duty 24-volt batteries
Honda generator
crowbars
pickaxes
snatch blocks
tins of grease
8 baulks of 6in x 4in timber
150 yards of wire rope
2 winches
2 hydraulic jacks
1 chain saw

During the fortnight I spent at Resolute the weather was constantly cold and foggy with snow falling and I became more and more worried that it might not be possible to return to the boat again that year. But, proving that luck does not

always run against one, the day that we had fixed for chartering the aircraft dawned bright and sunny with a light NW
wind. In addition to the two flight crew there would be Brian
and Glen from Narwhal plus myself and a very tough and
hard-working Inuit named Tony. One of the latter's assets was
that his mother lived at Cresswell Bay and he could call her up
by radio telephone to get a weather report. This was vital as I
would still have had to pay for the flight even if we were not
able to land at Fort Ross. Fortunately she was able to report
that the day was just as fine at Cresswell Bay and so, armed
with sandwiches and coffee thoughtfully supplied by Terry
Jesudason we lost no time in boarding the plane and setting
off.

It turned out to be as clear as a bell and we arrived at Fort
Ross around midday to find much better conditions than
when I had left. Tony used the Honda trike and trailer to
carry the first load of equipment while the rest of us were
walking down to the boat. On arrival Brian immediately
began searching around for suitable rocks to attach the hauling lines to, fortunately finding a perfect one. As soon as Tony
delivered them, we set up the two winches with snatch-blocks
and 6:1 purchases, securing the other end to the boat as
before. The greased timbers were laid out in front of the boat
to form a track so she would not dig into the ground. When
everything was ready, the Honda generator was connected to
the batteries and started up and finally the winches were
switched on.

To my intense relief the boat immediately began to move
forward onto the first greased timber and continued without
stopping as we laid out more timbers in front. We dragged her
about three boat's-lengths up the shore until she was well clear
of the water before calling a halt. In contrast to the earlier
effort, the operation went incredibly smoothly mainly thanks
to the very professional approach of Brian, Glen and Tony
and the whole thing was completed an hour and a half after

first switching on. Then as the others set about dismantling the equipment, I cleared the remaining water out of the boat and blocked up every aperture I could in the hope of keeping the snow out. Finally I fixed a sign to the cabin saying in both English and Inuit that she was not abandoned, in the hope of deterring any potential vandals who might pass by this remote spot.

Thanks to good planning the whole job went like clockwork and we were ready to take off again after approximately eight hours. The weather remained perfect throughout. I was now very much happier with the whole situation. Although the season had been wasted, I was safe, the boat was safe and I felt it was certainly possible to pick up the pieces the following year.

Next day the weather broke and the arctic winter was clamping down with its full savagery as I caught the flight out to Edmonton and home. As we cruised at 30,000 feet above the stormy Atlantic I was able to begin thinking about all the work that would be needed to get the expedition moving again the following year.

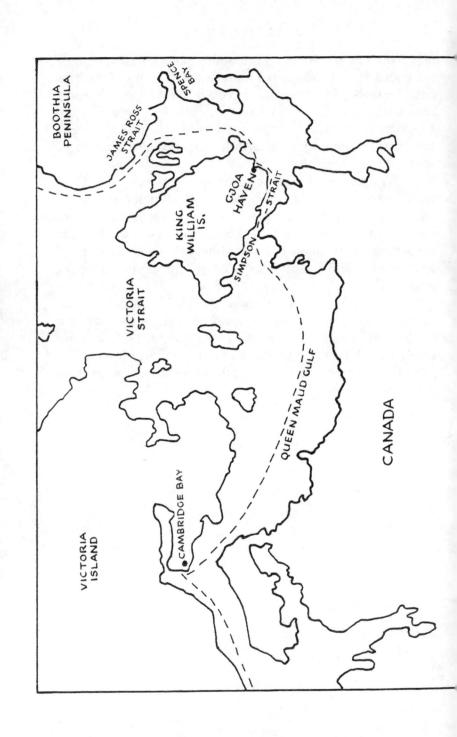

Chapter 7

Escape from Fort Ross

During the winter of 1987-88 I had time to consider what needed to be done to get my expedition moving again the following summer. At least this time I could feel confident that the boat would be safe in her shore berth above the high-water mark but there was still the problem of the persistent leaks. I therefore took advice on the best way of carrying out repairs. The real difficulty was that I would need to take with me absolutely everything needed to make these repairs, as once at Fort Ross there was no chance of popping round the corner to a hardware store. Working in the open and with no way of lifting the boat off the ground, I would be pretty restricted in what I could achieve.

Trying to undertake major boat-building work was really out of the question so I planned the best possible patch-up job I could. The first task was to assemble a mountain of equipment including glass-fibre, resin, copper sheets and tacks, Isoflex (a type of waterproof sealant), canvas, an electric

151

grinder, heaters, spare sea-cocks for the engine cooling system, spare piping, a wind generator and a big collection of tools in addition to what was already on board.

This was far too much to carry as personal baggage and it would obviously have to be freighted as far as Resolute. Following the problems with the radio in 1986, Plessey had been kind enough to air-freight the repaired set to Resolute in time for my arrival there in 1987, so I now asked them whether they would be prepared to arrange a new shipment of all the repair materials I had assembled. Initially they agreed and I delivered a car-load to their factory at Ilford. Three weeks later, when I called the firm to check that everything was going ahead I was told that they were unable to bear the cost of air-freighting this package because they had been badly affected by the recession and were having to make severe cutbacks. This put me in something of a quandary because having delivered all the items from Newcastle to Ilford I was not particularly keen to go and fetch them back again especially as I knew that Plessey's had a department that could professionally pack everything and forward it. After some discussion it was agreed that they would do the work if I paid the cost of £300. With hindsight I might have sensed that this arrangement was doomed to go wrong because it was not under my direct control but with so many other ends to tie up I was very happy to leave it in their hands.

Caroline very much wanted to see the Arctic for herself so we arranged that she would come with me to Fort Ross. There's no book of rules for motoring round the world in old lifeboats but I always felt it was reasonable to say I was 'singlehanded' provided no-one else was on board the boat when she was moving. There was never any possibility of doing such a trip without any kind of outside help in the way that one can in something like a single-handed yacht race. Therefore we did not feel it would be in any sense 'cheating' if Caroline helped me to work on the boat.

ESCAPE FROM FORT ROSS

We left London on 22 June with the maximum weight of personal baggage and flew to Montreal. Before leaving I telephoned Resolute and finding that the freight package had not arrived there, assumed it must be on its way. At Dorval Airport, Montreal, we made further inquiries in case the package was in the queue for an onward flight to Resolute but again there was no information. This was worrying but I was reluctant to cancel our own bookings to Resolute as we had special price return tickets and in any case the flight is nearly always full and it might have taken some time to find two more seats.

Having made the trip several times before, I knew what to expect but Caroline found it a fascinating flight, especially the fact that we left in darkness that gradually turned to orangey light as we crossed the Arctic Circle. With one intermediate stop at Frobisher Bay, the journey takes as long as flying from London to Montreal, which gives one some idea of the scale of the area. We were met at Resolute Airport by the Jesudasons who had kindly agreed to let us have a room for a few days. Their home is the nearest thing there is to a hotel in Resolute as they are so often involved in organizing expeditions.

The morning after arriving I began making phone calls in an effort to track down our freight package but there was absolutely no news of it. This was extremely frustrating because it made it so hard to decide whether to travel on to Fort Ross or wait at Resolute for the missing consignment. We spent several days waiting at Resolute hoping it would turn up, during which time we were able to explore the settlement more fully. The Hudson's Bay Company shop sells local carvings and we visited the little church which has a large polar bear skin spread out in front of the altar. Another attraction was the amazing aquarium of all the different varieties of fish, sea cucumber, anemones etc. that live in Resolute Bay and have been collected by the government scientist, Buster Welsh. Each day we visited the weather bureau to obtain the latest reports but eventually we decided to fly down to the boat with whatever materials could be bought or borrowed locally. John Goodman and Pat Gaulton at the Northern Transport maintenance depot were most helpful in rounding up items and had stored the batteries and other equipment over the winter. We next asked Bradley Air to arrange a Twin Otter flight to Fort Ross as soon as the weather was suitable.

This took place on 29th June and we spotted the boat immediately, looking very conspicuous in the snow. For me, this was a return to familiar territory but for Caroline it was all a new experience and she wrote in her diary:

"What a beautiful place – with the hills and the ice and the flatter places all different shades, all in basking sunshine. If you are going to get your boat stuck it is certainly a fantastic spot to do it!"

I have to admit that I had not really seen things in that light when I had been fighting to save the boat from becoming a total loss. We carried our stuff down to the boat, Caroline looking a little incongruous carrying several Sainsbury's bags, a briefcase and with a Browning rifle over her shoulder.

We were accompanied by Tony, the Inuit who had been so helpful when we hauled the boat out the previous year plus his young son Geoffrey and by a couple named Alfie and Virginia who said they were well-known independent video makers though the final result of their efforts tended to place them more in the realm of enthusiastic novices. We all plodded the two miles across the bay to where the boat was standing amid the snow-drifts. Apart from some peeling paint she looked in pretty good condition and, as Caroline remarked 'Unmistakably *Mabel*'.

In due course all our visitors made their way back to the Twin Otter and took off, and as the sound of the plane faded into the distance a wonderful silence took over. We were now totally alone – or so we thought – 250 miles from any kind of civilization. It is practically impossible for two people to sleep on board *Mabel E.Holland*, so we decided to set up house in one of the ex-Hudson's Bay Company huts – the same one that I had made use of before, which offered reasonable living accommodation, with sleeping platforms and a stove. There we bedded down pretty comfortably but early next morning I was woken by the sound of a loud rattling at the door.

I woke Caroline and told her to get dressed as quickly as possible and while we were both still struggling with all the layers of clothing there was a thud – up at the window in the door were two huge paws the size of dinner plates and a black nose while a pair of large black eyes peered in at us. Caroline swears that the bear turned first one eye and then the other to the glass for a better view. It flashed through my mind that when Caroline's mother had seen us off she had jokingly ordered me to look after her daughter and 'make sure she was not eaten by a polar bear.' We were both petrified as we knew that the cabin door would provide scant protection if the bear decided to have us for breakfast. It was for this very emergency that we had brought a rifle but with sinking heart I realized that the ammunition was on board the boat. Instead, with trembling hands I managed to take a photograph, using the last frame on the film.

After what seemed an eternity he lowered himself down and slowly wandered off behind the cabin while we kept him under observation through gaps in the planking. He had a good stretch and then to our alarm decided to come back for a second look. We decided to retreat to an upper platform inside the cabin where skins had hung when it had been a trading post. This had a tiny window directly above the door and in something of a panic we forced this open and stuck our heads out just as the bear came round the corner. Neither of us will forget the stare he gave us: if looks could kill we would have fallen down dead on the spot.

155

It is difficult to express just how menacing the bear was at such close range. They are very large and powerful animals and this one could easily have smashed down the door if it had been so minded. On another occasion I observed a polar bear grab a fully-grown seal weighing perhaps 300 lbs through an air-hole in the ice and just give it one violent shake over his shoulder and that was his meal. Seals have to come up to breathe every 40 seconds or so and keep these air-holes open all over the pack-ice. Hungry polar bears wait by the holes for a seal to surface and grab them with lightning speed when they do.

Fortunately for us, this particular bear decided to look elsewhere for breakfast and after shambling round outside the cabin, knocking over the oil drums I had arranged around the door, shuffled off in the direction of the boat. Here he found better pickings in the shape of Caroline's shopping bags (polar bears prefer Sainsbury's?) which he tore open and sampled, prior to chewing through some cables on deck and ripping a brand-new tarpaulin.

With that particular fright behind us, we both rolled up our sleeves and began work on the boat but thereafter remained extremely watchful and made sure that the rifle was never far away. We took as much equipment off as possible to improve the access and in so doing found some nasty-looking cracks in the aft compartment which were obviously at least partly responsible for the leaks. For the next few days Caroline concentrated on sorting out and cleaning the interior while I tackled the hull from the outside, grinding the paint off the suspect area of the stern. Neither was easy work: the whole interior had been saturated with a mixture of sea-water and diesel when the boat sank the previous year and it was a monumental job to scrub down all the surfaces and repaint them.

Working under the stern was not too much fun either thanks to the very limited clearance. I had to lie on my back in a stream of melt water that was continually trickling down from the higher ground beyond the shore, holding an electric grinder above my head. This resulted in becoming thoroughly wet and muddy on one side and thoroughly covered with paint and dust on the other. Even when the woodwork was exposed, it was virtually impossible to see how the water was getting in, due to the double-diagonal construction. My plan was to sand all the suspect area down to bare wood and then re-waterproof it as thoroughly as possible. This involved raking perished caulking out of the seams and fastenings and replacing it wherever possible with new epoxy filler. Due to most of the work being overhead I would not be able to use liquid resins to fill cracks and there were many areas where the wood was either too damp or too cold for the epoxy fillers to adhere and set properly. In these areas I planned to apply Isoflex, a rubberised roofing compound which will stick to slightly damp wood, and cover it first with canvas and then the copper patches that boatbuilders call 'tingles'. However these jobs would have to wait until the materials I had purchased in England arrived.

The weather was mostly good – though at a snap of the fingers an icy wind could blow and low cloud or fog descend – and one day we took time off to explore the area. We had brought photocopies of M'Clintock's book on the *Fox* expedition with us and decided to visit Port Kennedy (which he spelled 'Port Kenedy') where he had wintered. This involved quite a long trek of about 15 miles over rather boggy ground but on the way we were rewarded by coming remarkably close to a herd of eight musk-oxen and four young which were grazing on the moss and lichen. These primeval animals have roamed the Arctic for at least 90,000 years but during the past 100 years were hunted nearly to extinction. Fortunately they are now protected and are gradually recovering their numbers.

They are large, fine-looking animals with dark, chocolate-brown shaggy coats and coffee-coloured stockinged legs. They have two large horns, huge brown eyes and a mouth that is specially adapted for feeding in the ice. Apart from man, their predator is the Arctic Wolf and we were given a demonstration of their defence when we disturbed them; the adults forming a circle facing outwards around the young until they bolted at great speed up a steep shale embankment. The wolves can only hunt them successfully if they work in pairs or larger packs. We saw a pair in the distance and heard their mournful howl.

At Port Kennedy we failed to find the graves of the two members of M'Clintock's crew who were buried there: the engineer George Brands and the steward Thomas Blackwell but did come upon a cache of food tins with their crude lead soldering, plus glass flagons which were obviously from the M'Clintock era. Though very tempted, we decided not to bring anything away because it forms an important part of Canadian history and deserves to be left alone.

So engrossed did we become in our search of the area that we failed to notice that the rising tide was creating a kind of moat between the shore and the ice that still covered Port Kennedy. Walking right round the inlet would have involved a detour of many miles and so we had to take our courage in our hands and use some distinctly unstable blocks as stepping stones. However we eventually returned to the boat safely with nothing worse than wet trousers and boots.

Melting of the ice was at a much more advanced stage than at the same date the previous year and this gave me hope that I would at last be able to start moving again. One day, for instance, we clambered up the high ground overlooking Bellot Strait and could see clear water for several miles. This can also be a dangerous time of year as the short-cuts one is accustomed to taking across the sea suddenly become unsafe. Once when we were crossing a small bay, Caroline jumped onto a large piece of ice which rolled gracefully over, dropping her into the freezing water. It was lucky I was on hand as, weighed down with binoculars and camera, it would have been extremely difficult for her to climb out unaided.

Once back on dry land we jogged as quickly as we could to the boat to collect dry clothes and then to the hut so that Caroline – by now shivering violently – could change and warm up. A few days later I did a repeat performance myself, slipping between two slabs of ice that moved as I stepped from one to the other. I also discovered another way of writing myself off while attempting to burn the rubbish. One has to be as tidy as possible as food scraps or anything that smells of food will attract the bears and the idea was to put the rubbish in an empty 45-gallon fuel drum, add some fuel and set it alight. I must have been over-generous with the petrol because when I dropped a piece of lighted paper in the drum there was an impressive 'whoomph' and I found myself sitting on the ground several feet away minus eyebrows.

After a fortnight we had done about all we could to the boat but our daily radio calls brought no news of our freight from England. We therefore asked Bradley Air to come and collect us which was maddening, expensive and time-wasting but there seemed to be no choice. The aircraft arrived on the 12th July bringing Buster and Cathy Welsh from the Department of Fisheries who had taken the opportunity to come and see how we were progressing with the boat. On the way back to Resolute, we stopped off at Cresswell Bay long enough to do some fishing for Arctic Char which during the summer come swishing down from Stanwell-Fletcher Lake to spend two months in the sea.

From the air you could actually see a silver stream of the fish coming down into the estuary and after landing we could wade out in shallow water and cast into this stream. I caught five of these lovely fish and Caroline a couple more while Buster Welsh did better than either of us. We arrived back at

Resolute with a goodly supply of fresh fish which Cathy prepared and cooked. The rumour of good food spreads fast in a small community like Resolute and eighteen of us finally sat down to feast on Arctic Char, which we thought more delicious than salmon, at about 1 a.m. in the morning.

After a further round of fruitless telephone calls trying to trace the missing freight, we worked out that it would actually be cheaper to return to England and start all over again than stay put and try to order all the things we needed in Canada. Furthermore I was worried that we would simply run out of time waiting for items to be forwarded to Resolute. Feeling very frustrated we therefore took the next available flight home. We were back in England for two weeks which was mostly spent buying and assembling all the same stuff that we had already bought once before.

During this brief visit, I still did not manage to find out what had happened to the original consignment but to put the reader out of suspense I can reveal that I eventually discovered that the consignment had been sitting in a Customs shed in Edmonton waiting for an agent to clear it before it could continue to its destination. When this never happened, it was eventually returned and arrived on my doorstep in England a few days before Christmas.

At the beginning of August we were ready to set off again, with Caroline once again accompanying me. Not willing to risk losing any of our precious equipment a second time we decided the only thing to do was take it as passenger luggage and arrived at Heathrow Airport with an embarrassing mountain of stuff including four very heavy kitbags. To our amazement, Ward Air accepted the lot without extra charge and we took off feeling that perhaps my luck was changing at last.

Arriving back in Resolute on the 6th August we found the place so packed with expeditions that there were no beds available at the Jesudasons'. Fortunately we were able to find a room with Buster Welsh, who had been so helpful the previous year. He is a professor of Zoology who has visited the Arctic each summer for the past 20 years studying fish and pollution for the Canadian Fisheries Department. Buster was very excited because he had just taken delivery of a new 12m (40ft) fishing boat, which arrived on the deck of an ice-breaker.

As soon as the weather permitted, we flew down to Fort Ross as before and started work in earnest on the leaky hull. Before leaving I had arranged that the Narwhal team would fly in on the 16th August to launch the boat so we now had to make all haste to be ready in time. In the troublesome area of the propeller tunnels we used two different methods. On one side, I applied glass cloth and epoxy resin, while on the other Caroline got busy with Isoflex paint, covered by canvas and copper patches. There was also considerable work to be done on the decks which were leaking like the proverbial sieve and a total clean-up and reorganization below. We sanded off the decks and gave them two coats of the amazing Isoflex paint which was most successful and proved very hard-wearing. We also fitted up a diesel-fired heater in the engine-room to give some warmth below.

In our spare moments we built a stone cairn on the high ground behind the place where *Mabel* had wintered, and put inside it a card in a bottle giving details of our visit. Strangely enough we subsequently had a letter from someone who discovered this and was disappointed to find it referred to some very recent history. We were encouraged by the fact that there was incomparably more open water than the previous year and every chance that I would be able to make progress at last. The bay was virtually free of ice, though large pieces would flow in and out with the tide and wind. On Caroline's last evening at Fort Ross we sat together on a rock at the side of Bellot Strait and just quietly absorbed the beauty of the

161

place. We felt satisfied that we had done the best job we could on the boat and that she would now be reasonably seaworthy.

Next day the work party arrived to re-launch the boat – the same competent and hard-working people as before. This had to be a carefully-prepared exercise taking place at low water which on that day was at 0200 so we were working in the early dawn light. Oddly enough, it proved more difficult than hauling her out. I managed to drop a loop of steel wire rope over the large boulder offshore which I had selected earlier as a suitable anchor point but even with the powerful electric winches pulling through 6:1 purchases, *Mabel* was most reluctant to move. A number of times the 1in (25mm) diameter steel hawser running out to the boulder, parted dramatically under the strain and even with the winches working at their limit the boat only moved spasmodically in a series of abrupt jerks.

This was very nerve-racking as I was paying for the time that the aircraft spent sitting on the ground, in addition to the flights, while the cost of keeping the whole team waiting for a further twelve hours until the tide went down again would have been prohibitive. Eventually, after many difficulties, we managed to haul her down to a level where she would be floated by the incoming tide. As soon as the boat was as close to the water's edge as possible, the equipment had to be packed up and carried back to the aircraft which by now had been standing by for eight hours.

Caroline was flying out with the Narwhal party and was really sorry to leave as she had come to love the very special atmosphere of Fort Ross in spite of the occasional discomfort of living there.

Anyway, off went the plane, leaving me on my own at Fort Ross. I went back to the boat, the tide came in and she began to leak. In spite of all our work she seemed to be weeping through every joint – I could have wept myself. I calculated that about 200 gallons per day was finding its way aboard. At least I did not have to pump it out by hand as I now had an electric Jabsco pump which ran from the little Honda generator and I needed to use this at least once a day to keep the boat dry. At low water I searched carefully for tell-tale dribbles from the hull and fixed some more 'tingles' over suspect spots but only succeeding in cutting down the leak to about 150 gallons per day.

I was in a fever of impatience to get going but had to wait for four more days before I received a radio report that ice conditions were improving. During this time I established radio contact with John Bockstoce who was under way from Tuktoyaktuk in *Belvedere* and heading in my direction. John also told me about Rick Thomas, an adventurous yachtsman and climber who was attempting the Northwest Passage from east to west in his steel motor-sailer *Northanger*. He had sailed down Peel Sound and was now ahead of me.

On August 20th, 1988, I was finally ready to make my departure from Fort Ross which had been *Mabel's* home for almost exactly two years. Timing my departure to take advantage of the tide which runs at up to 8 knots through the strait I set off with considerable apprehension as there was a fair amount of ice choking the entrance. The difficulty lies in the fact that when the tide runs into the strait, it sucks in the loose ice which then tends to pile up against any obstruction. The most important of these is a large shoal to the west of Fox Island where the depth of water is less than 5m (16ft) in places. Much ice grounds on this shoal while to add to the difficulties, just a short way to the south of it in the middle of the deep water channel lies a semi-submerged rock, The Magpie, waiting to tear the bottom out of any unsuspecting vessel. To make it possible to pass safely between the shoal and The Magpie, transit marks are set up on Long Island but there is always the risk of a sudden drop in the visibility making these impossible to see.

Half way through the Strait is a small island, appropriately named Halfway Island. The distance from Magpie Rock to the western exit of the strait is 14 miles while the width is on average 730m (800 yards), with steeply-rising banks on either side which provide ideal nesting sites for the innumerable seabirds.

On reaching the shoal, my way was blocked by a raft of ice floes and more soon came sailing in astern. I was now entirely in the hands of the ice and the tide and for about an hour there were many anxious moments as *Mabel* groaned and flexed under the mounting pressure. Fortunately, the ice eventually forced its way through the gap, taking us with it and we began rushing through the narrow strait at quite an alarming speed.

In due course we popped out of Bellot Strait like a cork out of a bottle and emerged into the wider waters of Franklin Strait. A north-east wind was blowing the pack off the coast and a narrow lead opened up along the shore where there had been solid ice for more than two years. I had always known that this section of the passage, from Bellot down as far as Gjöa Haven, would be the hardest, as progress was completely dependent on the wind staying in the right quarter. If it changed while we were progressing down the unprotected west coast of the Boothia Peninsular, the ice would simple push back against the shore, pushing us with it.

My course took me south-westward past Gibson Island, Cape Sir F. Nicholson, Wrottesley Inlet, Cape Hodson and Graham Island after which I entered the Shortland Channel between the Boothia Peninsular and the islands of the Tasmania group. This was providential as just as I reached this channel, the wind swung round into the southwest, pushing the pack-ice back onto the coast and I was able to find a well-sheltered cove in which to anchor. While there, I was in radio contact with Rick Thomas who was in some difficulty at Weld Harbour where the ice had pushed *Northanger* ashore.

Though he and his crew were not in personal danger, he was worried in case they were pushed so far up that it would become impossible to refloat his boat. However thanks to the fact that she was fitted with a drop keel and retractable rudder, *Northanger* survived and was able to continue once the wind changed again. I also spoke to John Bockstoce who was at Oscar Bay, just a short way further south, waiting for the ice to break.

I remained holed up for two-and-a-half days until the wind went round and once more took the ice off shore. On the 23th I was on my way again, keeping very close to the shore as I made my way south past Pasley Bay where Sergeant Larsen had wintered in the *St Roch* during his 1941-42 passage, the first since Amundsen's. Now I could make good use of *Mabel's* shallow draught, motoring carefully along in water only about 1.5-2m (5-6ft) in depth and almost within touching distance of the shore.

On the 24th, after I passed Pasley Bay, the ice miraculously broke, opening up a lead through the James Ross Strait, and at about 2pm that day, between Cape Francis and Cape Bernard, *Belvedere* and *Mabel E.Holland* finally met. *Belvedere* dropped anchor and I was able to go alongside as there was only a very gentle breeze. We spent about 20 minutes exploring each other's boat after which we drank a toast to our health and successful completion of the Northwest Passage and each continued on our way.

I then continued into the James Ross Strait and shortly after passing Cape Victoria crossed tracks with *Vagabond II*, exchanging greetings and bottles with her crew. They in turn had passed *Northanger* about eight hours earlier. It really was extraordinary that of the very small number of yachts ever to transit the Northwest Passage, four should meet on the same day. At midnight that night I anchored close to St Thomas Island for a few hours rest while the tide was unfavourable, at the end of a long but exhilarating day.

Things were now becoming a little easier and I made excellent progress all next day through the St Roch Basin, passing Spence Bay and heading towards Rae Strait which is the fairly narrow stretch of water that separates the mainland from the Gibson Peninsular of King William Island. I then headed for Gjöa Haven which I reached at 8.30pm on the evening of the 25th.

It is a well-sheltered bay and as the weather was settled for the moment I was able to anchor and go ashore. Amundsen spent two years here and the magnetic observatory he set up has been turned into a small museum. The Hudson's Bay Company runs a trading depot here where there were some interesting native carvings for sale.

After this pleasant interlude, the next section to be traversed was Simpson Strait which is shallow, rocky, and has tides running at up to six knots! The charts are reasonably good but the undulating bottom creates powerful tide-rips which can carry a vessel into danger. The icebreakers put in place temporary buoys to mark the most dangerous shoals but there is no guarantee that these will not be dragged out of position by drifting ice so the main method of navigation is by transit beacons on the various small islands. For this one needs good visibility and I set off on the 26th in what seemed ideal conditions.

After anchoring briefly to check the tide I entered the strait but when I was about half way through, fog clamped down without warning. The magnetic compass was still far too vague to be of use and with daylight fading I was having to contemplate trying to anchor in a very unsafe area in a rising wind when I fortunately spotted a powerful flashing light from the DEW-line station at M'Clintock Bay. This gave me enough of a bearing to keep going through the hours of darkness which was fortunate indeed as the wind was up to 40 knots by the time we reached M'Clintock Bay, with *Mabel* virtually hidden by spray from the short steep waves. Arriving at about midnight, I was thankful to be able to drop the anchor, light the cabin stove and drop into an exhausted sleep.

The next section to be covered was Queen Maud Gulf – 150 miles of open but shallow water with very few landmarks and many reefs which I anticipated could be very tricky if there was a recurrence of strong wind combined with poor visibility especially as the magnetic compass was still virtually useless. But for once the wind dropped completely and for many hours I made excellent progress through a flat calm sea. It was too good to last, of course and the wind began to gradually build from the south as I approached Hat Island until it reached 40 knots or more, kicking up a wickedly short, awkward sea. Crashing through these made the boat leak more and every few hours I had to heave-to, start up the Honda generator and pump the bilges dry.

Entering the Requisite Channel, conditions were very rough but it was essential that my navigation should remain accurate in order to round the reef known as Amundsen Island before I could head up towards Jenny Lind Island where I hoped to find shelter. Just as the light was beginning to fade I was most surprised to see navigation lights approaching from astern. I wondered if my eyes were playing tricks as I thought I was in an area totally devoid of shipping but it turned out to be the NTCL tug *The Nuit Lang* towing a string of three supply barges. I spoke to the captain on the VHF and he told me he was on the way to Cambridge Bay and warned me of a gale forecast. Eventually I reached Jenny Lind Island in the dark but with a strong swell running into the bay I intended to enter, I was obliged to lie off very uncomfortably until first light when I was at last able to anchor and snatch some badly-needed rest.

Fortunately this bay gave ideal protection from the north and I remained there all the next day while the north-westerly gale screamed overhead. During the night the temperature dropped to −8°C but by morning the wind had moderated and I set off promptly for Cambridge Bay. By listening to the VHF chatter I learned that the icebreaker *Martha L.Black* was crossing my tracks on her way to Spence Bay. I called her up and found that my friend the ice observer Larry Solar was aboard. He told me that ice conditions along the Alaskan coastline were not good at all, with heavy polar pack right up to the shore due to the northerly winds. It is worth mentioning that it was later the same year that a pod of whales became trapped by the ice near Point Barrow and touched the hearts of many people who witnessed their struggle to survive when it was covered by TV news bulletins. However, it is important to remain optimistic in this part of the world and at that stage it was still possible for conditions to improve sufficiently to let me escape round Point Barrow that year.

In the early hours of the 30th August I reached Cambridge Bay and was again forced to lie off to await first light before entering because I could not see the transit marks that would guide me through the narrow channel. It is mostly very deep water there but I found a good anchorage at Freshwater Creek where I was very glad to reach shelter. It continued to blow at between 30 and 40 knots for the next four days during which *Mabel E.Holland* could only swing to her anchor though I did manage to row ashore and have a look round. One rather sad sight was an old hulk that turned out to be the *Maud* which Amundsen had used for his transit of the North*east* Passage. She had been bought by the Hudson's Bay Company for storage purposes but had been allowed to deteriorate over the years. Outside the bay, my old friend the *Pierre Radisson* was at anchor, on standby to escort a couple of commercial vessels from Point Barrow to Herschel Island.

While at Cambridge Bay I was delighted to meet up with Frederica Semotiuk whose husband Peter was with John Bockstoce on *Belvedere*. Both of them worked at the DEW-line radar station at Cambridge Bay and had been extremely encouraging friends via the radio when I had been in the depths of despair after the boat had sunk at Fort Ross. In fact, Frederica had been so struck by my predicament that she offered to pay the cost of one of the numerous Twin Otter flights I had been obliged to charter and it was a great pleasure to be able to thank her in person for this generous gesture.

The need to make progress before the sailing season ended was weighing heavily on my mind so I set off again from Cambridge Bay even though the wind was still blowing around 35 knots – a full gale. It was extremely rough and after only about five hours I was forced to seek shelter and anchor again. Next morning things were easier and I was able to snatch a few more miles of westward progress. This set the pattern for the next few days: battling through rough seas during the daylight hours and hoping to find a sheltered spot to anchor overnight. The navigation was too tricky and the weather too rough to be able to keeping going in the dark.

Nevertheless the miles were slowly ticking away and by 6th September I was out of the narrow straits inside Victoria Island and into the clearer waters of Amundsen Gulf. At this time I managed to speak on VHF with the cruise ship *Society Explorer* which was attempting to transit the Northwest Passage from west to east with a cargo of paying passengers. Tom Pullen was on board as her ice observer and I was overjoyed at the prospect of being able to meet again so we made a tentative arrangement to rendezvous at Cape Young the following day.

I anchored in the lee of this cape for the night and during the hours of darkness the wind howled, the thermometer dropped like a stone and fog set in making me conclude that there was very little hope that our meeting would take place but in the morning just as I had finished breakfast I stuck my head out, and to my astonishment there was the bright red hull of the ship, just coming to anchor only a few hundred metres away. I gave her master Captain Heinz Aye absolutely full marks for his skill and courage in piloting her there in such

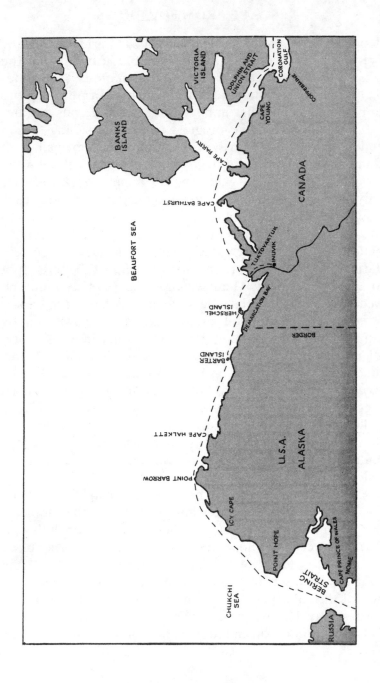

conditions. To my great delight he sent over an inflatable boat with an invitation to breakfast! This second hot meal, followed by a piping hot shower, was pure luxury and afterwards I was only too happy to give an impromptu talk to passengers about my protracted efforts to make my way through the Northwest Passage. By noon, I was back aboard *Mabel* while *Society Explorer* was on her way eastward again but I decided to stay put for a while as it was still blowing hard and foggy.

There was now a long section of exposed coastline with no convenient islands or headlands to shelter behind so I set off at first light on 8th September in quite reasonable conditions (only 20 knots of wind), keeping a few hundred yards offshore as usual. For once the weather stayed clear for just long enough allowing me to round the jutting headland of Cape Parry just as the wind started to pick up again from the north-east. I decided to make for Summer Harbour on Booth Island and reached it at dusk in very difficult conditions. It gave excellent shelter from the ice but the wind was still shrieking across it at around 40 knots and the holding ground for the anchor turned out to be very poor. Several times during the night I had to re-anchor but the trouble was that in darkness and a violent storm it was pretty well impossible to know where the dangers lay. At one stage during the night when it was pitch black and snowing, the boat dragged her anchor to within a few metres of the shore. My predicament was that if I went forward to recover the anchor, the period of time between it breaking out of the ground and my being able to secure it and rush back to the engine controls might well prove fatal and in any case I had little idea which way safety lay. It was perhaps the most anxious and exhausting night of the whole passage and when dawn came, revealing the shocking sight of jagged rocks no more than ten metres away, I realized that I had come extremely close to disaster.

From time to time I had been talking on the radio to Rick Thomas who now told me that *Northanger* had come to a dead stop a short way beyond Herschel Island which is on the west side of the Mackenzie delta. From the various ice-breakers we were hearing that conditions were very bad along the North Shore of Alaska and that it was most unlikely that we would be able to round Point Barrow and reach the Bering Strait that year. Being thoroughly unwilling to leave the boat in some remote and exposed position again, I decided to make for Tuktoyaktuk, a settlement at the mouth of the Mackenzie and now only a day's motoring ahead. I knew that Bockstoce's *Belvedere* had been hoisted out of the water there and I imagined I could arrange the same thing for *Mabel*. At the same time, Rick Thomas was visited by Canadian Rangers who told him that *Northanger* was in a dangerously exposed position and added rather dramatically that his whole crew might die if they remained there. Rick himself was quite prepared to take the risk of over-wintering on board the yacht but his Kiwi crew were less than delighted by this prospect and urged him to back-track to 'Tuk'.

After the awful night at Summer Harbour I set off in very mixed conditions of drifting fog towards Franklin Bay. As I approached, the 'Smokey Hills' were much in evidence. The smoke comes from exposed bituminous shale which burns spontaneously and gives off a strong sulphurous smell. Cape Bathurst, on the west side of Franklin Bay is the most prominent feature in the area and in theory I could have saved some distance by passing through the Snowgoose Passage inside Baillie Island but with a big swell and restricted depth I decided that discretion was advisable and went round it.

I was now heading for Tuktoyaktuk and as I entered the Mackenzie delta the most extraordinary change overcame the weather: the wind dropped away entirely, the sun came out and the temperature soared. By 11th September I was safely moored alongside the jetty of the Northern Transportation Co. at Tuktoyaktuk. But although I waited there for another four days in the hope of a dramatic change in conditions along the Alaskan coast, this was not to be and the experts stated quite categorically that they foresaw no more 'melt days' that season. Meanwhile I had been talking to the people at the transport depot who advised me that it would really be better to motor 100 miles up the Mackenzie River to the town and freight depot of Inuvik which has more facilities and an airport.

John Bockstoce had given me an introduction to Jim Hamblin who, as well as being a Director of Northern Transportation Co Ltd (NTCL) came originally from Whitley Bay near Newcastle so was a fellow 'Geordie'. I spoke to him on the telephone and he put me in touch with the manager of the Inuvik freight depot, Rick Connors who proved most helpful and agreed that the boat could be hoisted out there and I passed on the same information to Rick Thomas. At Tuktoyaktuk there was a makeshift cradle which John Bockstoce had had made for *Belvedere* when he laid her up there and he had already suggested I might like to use it. Now the NTCL people very kindly said they could put this on one of their barges and take it up the river to Inuvik.

Two days of pleasant, easy motoring up the mighty Mackenzie was a relief from the anxieties of the ice-girt coast. The warmer water of the river creates its own micro-climate with abundant vegetation and even some small trees along the banks. Arriving at Inuvik I received a friendly welcome from the people at the freight yard. It is built to handle standard shipping containers which are loaded onto barges by a machine like a giant fork-lift truck. As this was the only machine available at the yard and they didn't have any slings I set to work to make up strops using the boat's own mooring warps. When I was satisfied with the cats-cradle of rope I had created, the Lectro Lift machine was driven to the side of the dock and we passed the loops of rope over its arms with halved logs to stop the metal cutting through them. It could easily lift *Mabel's* weight but there was some fairly alarming creaking

173

and groaning as the lines took the strain. Once clear of the water, the machine trundled gently across the yard and set *Mabel* down on the waiting cradle. And that was it!

A day later *Northanger* appeared and went through the same process though she was harder to hoist because of her deeper shape. The two boats were chocked up alongside and the extremely helpful staff built a stockade of shipping containers around them. The yard is closed during the winter and this stockade would give protection both from the weather and any visiting bears or souvenir-hunters. With the boat now in a completely safe situation I felt very much happier and was able to 'winterize' her properly by draining down the engine-cooling, removing all drain-plugs and so on.

Although I had failed to complete the Northwest Passage, I had escaped the icy embrace of Fort Ross and covered a distance of 1,500 miles in just three weeks. It had been hard going but compared to the previous autumn, I felt that the whole situation was now infinitely better and returned home to England a very much happier man.

n1 9778
797.1 m -S
710.9163 C

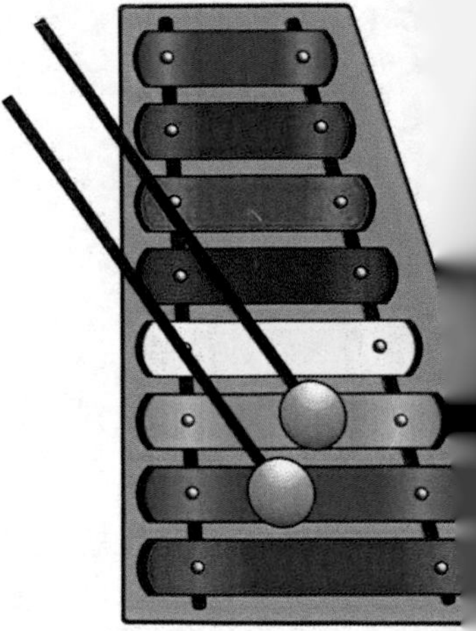

Chapter 8

The passage completed

THE WINTER of 1988/9 was one of the coldest on record in the Arctic, with temperatures falling to −100°C (−148°F), but as *Mabel E.Holland* was in a completely safe situation, with all the water drained out of her engines and bilges, this intense cold was of no special concern and may even have helped the natural drying-out process by 'freeze-drying' the hull. Nevertheless this extreme cold did not augur well for an early break-up of the ice the following summer. The previous year, 1988, had been a very bad one in the Western Arctic with heavy polar pack being driven ashore by constant northerly winds all the way from Herschel Island to Point Barrow.

This part of the Passage tends to be very shallow so it only takes a small amount of ice to block it, the main pressure points being Herschel Island, Barter Island, Cape Halkett and finally Point Barrow itself. I was in regular correspondence with Tom Pullen through the winter and also obtained helpful advice from John Bockstoce who had spent a considerable time in the area during his protracted west-east passage but it was pointless to fret over the situation in advance, as one always has to be an optimist when dealing with the Arctic.

During the winter months I was able to plan my strategy for the coming season; with the boat now so much more accessible it was possible to undertake a much more extensive repair programme. Uppermost in my mind was the fact that even after escaping from the Northwest Passage, 20,000 sea-miles still lay ahead so it was obviously essential for the boat to be made fully seaworthy.

Mabel E.Holland had been chocked up on the ex-*Belvedere* cradle at the NTCL depot at Inuvik, giving me about 75cm (2ft 6ins) of working space under the hull – a vast improvement compared with having to lie prone in the slush at Fort Ross. I wanted to strip the entire hull back to bare wood and give it a completely new covering in an effort to stop the leaks but this was not going to be easy as the underside of the hull had been ribbed or 'castled' with stringers to protect it while being dragged over the shingle during her lifeboat service. The gap between these stringers was only about three inches, making it difficult to use the usual type of power-sander.

After talking to various experts, I found a lightweight air-driven tool fitted with a 2in (4.8cm) sanding plate for which abrasive disks in various grades were available from the 3M Company. I had already ascertained that I could obtain a portable air compressor in Inuvik. International Paints very kindly helped me with a supply of epoxy fillers, fast-drying paints and antifouling and I paid a visit to SP Systems in Cowes to obtain their advice on the best epoxy resins and cloths to use. I also approached Winthrop Laboratories about the use of their Isoflex paint which is really designed for waterproofing roofs of buildings but had proved very effective when applied to *Mabel's* leaky decks. After speaking to all these experts I settled on a plan to remove all the old paint and filler, glass over the most suspect areas, refill all seams and apply four coats of epoxy paint followed by three coats of Isoflex followed by two coats of antifouling.

The next problem would be to transport all this stuff to Canada. After the previous year's fiasco I was determined to take it all with me as passenger baggage but this called for a certain degree of subterfuge as airlines tend to throw up their hands in horror at the mention of paint. I therefore had six glass-fibre canisters made, into which I slid the tins of paint before sealing them up with glass and resin so that you could not look at the contents without actually cutting the canister open. I had obtained a complete set of forty US charts of the coast from the Mackenzie Delta to the Bering Strait and I wrapped these round the canisters of paint to give them a more innocent appearance. The only trouble was that each one weighed 18kg (40lbs) in addition to which I had the sander, a large supply of discs for it and a number of other spare parts and bits and pieces, on top of my own kitbag.

On 22 June 1989 I presented myself at Heathrow Airport with some feelings of apprehension over my illicit cargo of paint and wondering what large sum I would be paying for excess weight. However at this juncture a guardian angel fluttered by, as it turned out there was a booking problem with the flight I was supposed to be on and the airline staff asked whether I would mind transferring to another. I was happy to do so and to show appreciation of this flexibility, my groaning trolley-load of baggage was whisked onto the aircraft with no further questions asked.

The flight arrived at Inuvik at some unearthly hour of the morning but in June this part of the world enjoys 24-hour daylight. The freight yard was now back in action and I was able to hire a taxi to carry all my stuff from the airport right to the boat, and although the driver muttered about his springs, this was almost laughably simple compared with the extreme difficulty and expense of getting to the boat the previous year.

The protective corral of containers had recently been removed and the boat was sitting there exactly as I had left her the previous October.

I made my number with Jeanne Lycett, the new manageress of the freight depot who was quite happy for me to stay on board the boat and work in the yard and I also greeted Bud, the Lectro Lift operator, who had been so helpful with hoisting the boat out. Rick Thomas and his New Zealanders were already there, working hard to make *Northanger* ready for launching. I looked over the boat with Rick and found her surprisingly dark and bit cramped down below, though strong and well-equipped. They in turn looked over *Mabel* and like everyone else, could not believe how I managed to live in such a restricted space.

Although I was on very good terms with Rick and his Kiwis, he made it quite clear that his aim was for *Northanger* to become the first British vessel to complete the Northwest Passage and realistically, there was not much I could do about it. Even if we both set off at the same time, he would have been able to push on harder due to his greater manpower and in any case I had decided not to launch the lifeboat until I was completely satisfied with her seaworthiness.

The day after arriving, after I was rested and unpacked, I got hold of an air-compressor and braced myself for the long job of stripping the hull. The extraordinary thing about the Mackenzie is that it has its own climate and at the end of June it was hot and dry with temperatures in the 65-75 Fahrenheit range (18-24°C). There was no trace of ice in the river and the biggest problem was the swarms of mosquitos which are especially trying whenever there is not much wind.

To cope with these conditions I would get up wearing shorts and a sweat-shirt plus long woollen socks as a protection against the mosquitos. When ready to begin work I would add disposable overalls including a hood, plus goggles and a dust-mask when sanding. In spite of regularly spraying my ankles and wrists with mosquito repellent, I was severely bitten. Provided the weather was not too warm, I could put in 10-12 hours of work a day before breaking for a meal at 7 or 8pm. I then allowed myself an hour's walk to relax before retiring to my bunk on board. It was hot and stuffy in the cabin due to the need to keep the doors and windows shut against the mosquitos.

Work on the hull kept me busy for the next six weeks. The first few weeks were spent sanding off every scrap of paint and when this was done I would rake out perished filler from the seams and also pick filler out from the multitude of hull fasteners. Water had been seeping in by both of these routes and especially the latter as I discovered that a number of wood-screws and other fasteners had broken. Seams one can re-fill but broken screws are especially troublesome as it is practically impossible to pull them out. After seams and screw-holes had been carefully brushed out and cleaned, I would refill them with epoxy filler, sand off and then start applying the various coats of paint. It took approximately one whole day to apply a coat of paint so ten days were taken up on this operation alone. During the whole of this time the weather continued hot and dry with very little rain. Apart from being uncomfortable at times, it was ideal for applying the various epoxy paints which had to be done to a strict timetable in order to achieve the proper adhesion between coats.

Rick Thomas was able to have *Northanger* launched at the end of June and then continued fitting her out and loading supplies and fuel. Although it was really too early in the season, Rick and his crew decided to leave Inuvik during the first week of July and make their way down the Mackenzie in an effort to reach Herschel Island. Using Herschel as a jumping-off point they would try to make progress to the west whenever the opportunity presented itself. While both boats were still at the depot we used to take turns to call the

Canadian Coastguard each day for the latest ice reports and after *Northanger* had left, Rick would call in by radio to hear the news. By the third week of July the ice reports began to become much more promising.

By 25th July I had at last completed all the work on the hull of *Mabel E.Holland* and also changed the seals on the prop shafts and serviced the engines. I therefore asked Bud to launch her, again using the mighty Lectro Lift container forklift which is able to carry up to 80 tonnes. As before, the difficulty lay in slinging the boat using her own warps and some calculation was required to make sure these were the correct length as the arms of the lift could be lowered only as far as ground level. Thanks mainly to the great skill and care of Bud, the operation went off without a hitch and *Mabel* was soon lying alongside the quay.

An anxious vigil followed as I waited to see whether she still leaked but after 24 hours I was overjoyed to find the bilges virtually dry. Unfortunately it was a little premature to conclude that the problem was completely solved as she was not yet loaded and the fuel alone would add four tons and push her a further 5 inches down in the water. When everything was on board, the familiar trickles of water began to reappear in various compartments but nothing like as much as before. At worst, she leaked around a gallon an hour, and with the additional pumps I had fixed up this was easy to control and not a real worry.

Fuelling up was straightforward as a tanker could be driven right to the quayside and fill the main tanks by hose. I filled all the cans on dry land and then had a hard day's work lowering them to the deck and stowing them. With the lifeboat fuelled, stored and watered, the provisions checked and the charts and log-book sorted, I was ready to say goodbye to the ever-helpful staff at NTCL and get under way on the evening of 28th July. I had received a very encouraging ice report from my old friend Larry Solar, who predicted a good navigational season and set off down river with high hopes.

With a favourable current of 2 knots I was able to motor along sedately absorbing the scenery on either side. The banks of the river are green and shrubby but as soon as one moves away from the river the prospect becomes very bleak – the 'barren lands' that were such a barrier to exploration. After anchoring for the night near the mouth of the river, I got under way early on the 30th, soon encountering a short, awkward swell in the shallow estuary. Even ten miles off-shore, the depth is no more than 6.7m (22ft), making it a place to avoid in bad weather.

The visibility was excellent as I headed out past Pullen Island, named after Tom Pullen's great-grandfather who had discovered it while searching for signs of the Franklin Expedition. He sailed 700 miles in an open naval whaler from the Bering Strait before returning overland. The island looked quite inviting, being covered with green vegetation and having a log cabin and flag-pole. Next I rounded Hooper Island and Pelly Island, named after my co-author David Pelly's great-great-great-grandfather Sir John Henry Pelly, Governor of the Hudson's Bay Company and Deputy Master of Trinity House.

At this stage the pack-ice was a comfortable four miles or so away on my starboard side as I headed for Herschel Island, 100 miles to the west. At long last I was able to start using my Neco autopilot which released me from the chore of needing to be constantly at the wheel. This made life immensely easier as it meant I could navigate, prepare food, pump the bilges, check the engines, transfer fuel and all the other thousand and one shipboard tasks without needing to stop each time. Unlike Rick Thomas with his crew of six, I did however still need to either anchor or just stop and drift in order to sleep.

Although the weather remained reasonably good, it became steadily colder as the influence of the Mackenzie's outflow lessened and the familiar menace of fog soon made its presence felt. The ice grew steadily closer to the coast and on my second day out I began to pass some really heavy polar pack which loomed up eerily out of the mist. That night I managed to establish radio contact with *Northanger* which was then at Barter Island only about 120 miles away, so their three-and-a-half week start had not gained them all that much distance. Perhaps the tortoise would have a chance of catching the hare after all.

In the early hours of 31st July I arrived at Pauline Cove, Thetis Bay, Herschel Island and entered via what the chart described as 'The Workboat Passage' for which the maximum draught is 1.2m (4ft). The weather had now changed completely, being very cold with 20 knots of wind from the northwest. Navigation the previous night had been difficult with thick fog and up to 6/10ths concentration of heavy pack-ice. Once in the cove I anchored and slept, awaking to find the weather had changed for the better once more, allowing me to have a proper look at the island.

Herschel, which was named by Franklin after the astronomer who discovered Uranus, has an interesting history as it was a great gathering point for the whaling fleets of the 19th Century. Eventually it became a honky-tonk frontier town with up to 2,000 inhabitants, complete with imported ladies of easy virtue, and as a result was one of the first posts for the Royal Canadian Mounted Police when the force was formed. Nowadays it is a nature reserve and a few of the remaining buildings from the whaling era are being preserved.

One of the wardens came out in a rubber boat and invited me ashore to look round. There are no trees but the ground is covered with cotton-grass which at least gives a green appearance and there were masses of bright-coloured wildflowers which have to rush through their entire life-cycle in the few weeks of the arctic summer. If you dig in the ground, however, you reach permafrost at a depth of about 22cms

(9ins) which is presumably why no large plants can survive. The frost causes the ground to swell and heave and for this reason many of the 19th century memorials are left leaning over at crazy angles while graves have to be re-dug to stop their contents coming to the surface. I was taken to see an 'ice-house' – a large dug-out in the permafrost inside which the temperature remains at a constant −15°C (5°F). Any kind of food such as locally-caught fish can be stored in this natural deep-freeze. In the sunshine, Herschel was tranquil and it was difficult to imagine it as a tavern of the Arctic. The wardens invited me to share a supper of barbecued herring and delivered me back to the boat at midnight to conclude a fascinating visit.

The 1st of August was another fine, sunny day and I left as I had arrived through the Workboat Passage and continued parallel to the shore. The edge of the pack-ice was now just a few hundred yards away on my starboard side but I was able to make good progress, reaching my next objective, Demarkation Bay in the early evening. On the way I passed the DEW Line radar station at Komakuk Beach where two ex-SAS soldiers Mike Jacques and Mike Marriott had left their 4.9m (16ft) sailing boat the previous autumn. They started from Nome, Alaska and were hoping to reach Pond Inlet on Baffin Island but lack of sponsorship forced them to abandon the expedition after 1988 and I gathered the boat was simply left there.

After a night at anchor in Demarkation Bay I set off again in thick fog. It is amazing that conditions that might previously have seemed unacceptably hazardous: motoring along a narrow channel between the ice and the shore in bad visibility and with the constant threat of bad weather, now seemed relatively normal or even straightforward. I had been warned that getting past Barter Island might be difficult but fortunately it was calm when I arrived there and was able to thread my way through a collection of really massive blocks of ice without too much difficulty. So far, progress had been excellent and I took the opportunity of anchoring for a good rest at Bernard Harbour, on Barter Island, prior to tackling the long and potentially tricky section of coast to Point Barrow.

I was now in US coastal waters and traversing the 'North Slope' of Alaska which is well-known as one of the world's most important oil-fields. The coast is low and featureless with a series of shallow lagoons along it and as a result navigation was far from easy. I set off on 3rd August in snow and average visibility but kept up a good mileage thanks to less dense pack-ice. Having decided to take a short-cut by going outside the Maguire Islands, I was shaken when *Mabel E.Holland* went hard aground without warning as I came up to the Stockton Islands. With a strong west-going tidal stream carrying us onto the shoal, it was hard to decide whether to push ahead in the hope of bouncing over the shoal or try to back off against the strong current. Luckily, while I was thinking about this, she freed herself but I did wonder what I would have done, had we ended up high and dry on a shoal miles from anywhere. Apparently the depth can be as much as 1.2m (4ft) less than indicated on the chart in this area, depending on wind direction.

Having survived this fright I continued past the impressive oil installations of Prudhoe Bay whose flood-lit gantries provided an unmistakeable land-mark. After passing Midway Islands, in order to have a change of scenery I thought it would be fun to go inside the Jones Islands and take the Simpson Channel through the inshore lagoon. This brought me out into Harrison Bay with the next objective Cape Halkett. I could hardly believe my luck as the wind remained light and there was tolerable visibility with just occasional fog and snow showers. Keeping my fingers crossed, I kept going with short stops for rest, all the way to Point Barrow which I reached at 8.30pm on 5th August.

184

Reaching Barrow was a great psychological boost as it is the most northerly point of Alaska and the real corner-stone of the Northwest Passage. Although I still had some way to go before completing the Passage at Bering Strait, my course would always be to the south in future and one might reasonably expect that ice would become less of a threat. Unfortunately Point Barrow itself is low-lying and unimpressive with just a flag-pole to mark the entrance to the Arctic.

Rather than enter the harbour, I anchored in the shelter of the sand-spit and had a good night's rest. The following day was flat calm with a strong smell of fish in the air so I decided to continue immediately. Whales dived around the lifeboat as she sliced smoothly through the mirror-calm sea and I passed what appeared to be a dead minke whale floating belly up.

As I continued on my course down towards Cape Lisburne, I had a night of drama, as the papers say. I had dozed off as *Mabel E.Holland* motored steadily along under autopilot, and woke with a start when the starboard engine came to an abrupt stop, accompanied by a loud 'clonk' from the starboard propeller tunnel. Looking over the side, I could see nothing amiss and it was now time to make use of one of the lifeboat's most ingenious features, the propeller inspection hatches. By removing a water-tight plate in the cockpit floor one can look down through an aperture at the propeller. Lifeboats run a high risk of getting ropes or wreckage entangled in their props and many a tricky situation has been avoided by using these hatches.

On opening the starboard hatch, I could see that a large tree-trunk had been drawn into the tunnel and was firmly wedged in the propeller. The prop shaft was reluctant to turn in either direction and I spent something like two hours shoving and levering the log with various instruments before it finally came free. But no sooner had I got under way again than the port engine lost power and died. This time the trouble was water in the fuel which necessitated clearing the filter bowls and renewing the cartridges. When both engines were once more running properly, I noticed that the satellite navigation receiver had failed. I had my trusty sextant and tables in reserve but they are no use in fog.

Just after midnight on 7th August I rounded Icy Cape and 24 hours later I was abeam of Cape Lisburne, the last major landmark before the Bering Strait, with the visibility deteriorating rapidly. That evening I was able to make radio contact with *Northanger*; Rick Thomas reported that they were approaching the straits in good sailing conditions. Although they were no more than 300 miles ahead, it was clear that short of an accident, they were going to get through first.

During the 9th, a couple of big tugs loomed up out of the mist, towing barges northward. I was able to call them up on the VHF and obtain a position check, which was 66 degrees, 52 minutes North, 167 degrees, 39 minutes West: just inside the Arctic Circle. That night there was proper darkness for a couple of hours, the first I had experienced since arriving at Inuvik at the end of June. At the same time the wind was building up steadily to 25 knots from the south and the visibility continued to be bad. The Northwest Passage was not going to release me without a final struggle.

Approaching the Bering Strait on 10th August 1989, the weather continued to deteriorate rapidly with the southerly wind building up to gale force and continuing thick fog. When I finally reached the conclusion of my long battle with the Northwest Passage, there was absolutely nothing to see and only my dead reckoning calculation plus a dubious position on the SatNav to assure me that I really had made it at last. But the dismal conditions could not quell the feeling of elation that I felt: *Mabel E.Holland* was the 46th vessel of any kind to transit the passage, the second British vessel, and I was the first person to have done the complete passage single-handed. Still ahead lay the opportunity to become the first to complete a circumnavigation via the Northwest Passage.

Although the straits are only 45 miles wide, I never saw any of the land on either side: neither Cape Prince of Wales, Alaska nor Cape Dezhneva on the Russian side or any of the Diomede Islands and I continued to motor completely blind until shortly before arriving at Dutch Harbour on Unalaska Island in the Aleutians which curve out in a sickle shape from the Alaska Peninsular. The SatNav had started to work again but without a sun-sight to confirm my position I could not tell if it had re-set itself correctly and the whole of this 800 mile passage was done on dead-reckoning. It was not until I was within five miles of Unalaska that the mists suddenly lifted to present a dramatic view of the magnificent island scenery with snow-capped mountains gleaming in the sun and green pastures on the lower slopes.

The rest of this story must now be quickly told even though it involved a long and often difficult voyage round the World in the faithful but sorely-tried *Mabel E.Holland*. I entered Dutch Harbour on 15th August and went through the US entry formalities with two helpful ladies; Karen of Customs and Trish the Immigration Officer who did not quite know what to think about my strange-looking craft or my story of having come from England in her. I had not been able to make any radio calls from the Bering Strait so a first priority on getting ashore was to telephone home with the good news that I had completed the Northwest Passage at last. ITN carried the story on their national news bulletins and there was considerable coverage in the newspapers.

Feeling in need of some rest and recuperation after my virtually non-stop dash from Herschel Island, I remained for five days during which I refuelled and sorted out various jobs on board. Dutch Harbour has a frontier atmosphere and boasts more bars and night-clubs per head of population than most places on earth. One of these, the Elbow Room is known for the fact that a brawl can be guaranteed on most nights. When I arrived, the harbour was packed with fishing boats which had arrived for the 'cod season' which lasts for exactly 24 hours during which everyone works non-stop to make the best of this brief bonanza.

A number of people were very helpful at Dutch Harbour including the manager and staff at the Delta Western fuel dock and the crew of the fish factory ship *Pacific Glacier* who kindly made up some stainless steel brackets so I could fix two hand bilge-pumps to the engine-room bulkhead. A lady named Nancy let me use her bath and washing machine while Trish of Immigration took me on a sight-seeing tour of the island. One day a chap gave me half a bucket of cooked crabs' legs which were first class as the fish and crabs from this area are some of the best in the world.

From Dutch Harbour I telephoned my secretary Beryl Turner who had taken on the job of voyage coordinator, in the hope that she could help solve a problem over my next destination, Midway Island. This is a US military base and the Commander in Chief, Pacific Fleet had refused my request for permission to call there. The alternative was Hawaii, many hundreds of miles further east and this would have made the following leg of the journey much longer and more difficult.

I asked Beryl to pull every string possible and she thought of the MP for Tynemouth, Neville Trotter who had given me much support on previous voyages. Unfortunately Neville was on holiday with his family at a remote cottage in the Lake District with no telephone but his secretary managed to persuade the local farmer to give him a message. In spite of this interruption of his holiday, Neville kindly called the US naval representative in London, Vice-Admiral Ilg who in turned contacted the Pentagon in Washington. Twenty-four hours later, this high-level activity was rewarded and permission was received from the Pentagon. As a bonus, Admiral Ilg offered to forward my mail to Midway through US military channels, a welcome surprise when I arrived there.

This vital piece of news was the signal to send me on my way from Dutch Harbour on 19th August, though not without a very frightening incident when I blundered into a dangerous tide-rip off Unalga Island. With an eight-knot tidal stream against her, *Mabel E.Holland* was suddenly among 3.6m (12ft) high seas with vertical faces that just cascaded onto the deck. I had twenty very anxious minutes and could have been in serious trouble if the engines had failed at this moment. Eventually the tide eased and we broke free as I cursed myself for not being more thorough in checking the tide tables.

Once through the island chain, I set course for Midway, 1,600 miles to the south-west. The first few days were rough but after the half-way point it calmed down and the temperature began to increase dramatically. In just a few days I seemed to have sailed from the Arctic to the Tropics. The propeller hatch came into use again when I caught part of a fishing net in the port prop at 41 degrees North while passing through an immense collection of flotsam and rubbish that seemed to be held in a local current.

On the last day of August I entered the harbour at Midway Island to be greeted by the harbour master Captain Jerry Falls. It was extremely hot and humid ashore and a great pleasure to go into the Captain's air-conditioned office to go through the entry formalities. As usual with US authorities, once they have decided you are acceptable, they cannot do too much for you and I was amazed to be given the use of a comfortable bedroom and bathroom in an air-condition barrack block for the length of my stay, including use of a communal washing machine.

Midway is a small coral island at the north-west tip of the Hawaiian chain which was important mainly as a refuelling point for aircraft crossing the Pacific. It is a breeding ground for the albatross or 'Goony Bird' and I could not see what was supposed to be so secret about the place. Nevertheless there was considerable consternation one day when a light aircraft arrived completely unannounced containing an English couple called Mike and Anne Wright who were flying around the world. Eventually these extra 'limeys' were made welcome too, and allowed to stay for a few days before flying on to the Aleutians.

The next stage, to Port Moresby in Papua New Guinea, was a long and arduous one of 4,000 nautical miles. I filled every tank and can with the greatest care until the decks were almost awash with the weight of over 1,000 gallons of diesel. Carrying the cans in the wringing humidity was more exhausting than anything I had done in the Arctic. Life being fairly uneventful at Midway, there was quite a gathering to see me off on 8th September and I was presented with a bottle of whisky to see me on my way.

The long, long passage to Port Moresby took 23 days during which the remarkable old Gardner engines, which, remember, were 30 years old and had already been round the world once, never missed a beat unless I shut them down for an oil-check. Instead, it was me that was feeling the strain of endlessly heaving fuel-cans on deck and decanting their contents into the tanks in heat that often reached 100°F (38°C) inside the boat. On the 12th September I managed to make contact on the 'ham' frequencies with Matt ZL4 JO who has been my most faithful companion on the airwaves during four circumnavigations of the world. From this time onwards I was able to speak to Matt daily and make myself feel a bit better by having a good grumble about the heat.

Having passed through the Gilbert Islands in the dark without seeing anything, I crossed the Equator on 21st September and altered course towards the Bouganville Strait between Bouganville and Choiseul Island in the Solomons. Passing through the strait on the 26th the wind increased rapidly to force 6 with a lumpy, awkward sea which forced me to keep the boat closed up, increasing the heat and humidity inside still further.

The most tricky part of this long passage was rounding the end of Papua New Guinea where there are numerous small islands, and low-lying reefs with strong tidal streams running between them. In the early hours of 29th September I passed Panaete Island and ran parallel with the reef for ten miles before passing the tide rip of the West Passage to set course for Jomard Island. Unfortunately it became clear I would not reach Jomard in daylight and it was essential to steer an accurate course in the narrow passage. The chart was pock-marked with wrecks and I had no wish to add to the total. At about midnight I finally passed Jomard in extremely difficult conditions of pitch-black tropical night with heavy rain squalls and a 6m (20ft) swell and strong wind. I never saw the light on the island and it was a huge relief to break out into the clear waters of the Coral Sea. After a further day of rough weather I entered the Basilisk Passage into Port Moresby, to end one of the longest non-stop passages I had done in *Mabel E.Holland*.

Mabel was now back in familiar territory as we had visited Port Moresby in 1984 and had several friends there. On the previous occasion, they were just starting work on a new marina and now it was not only finished but completely full so that I had to anchor off near a smart Laurent Giles yacht named *Pittulis Pride* whose owner Malcolm Rose I had met just before setting off from England in 1986. I spent several days relaxing and socializing including two very agreeable trips into the cooler air of the Highlands with John Bray, an old friend who is a solicitor there. Through a contact at Swire Shipping, Andrew Craig-Bennett, I was offered some fuel from the ship *Kurari Chief* and spent the best part of a day while they ran the fuel through their purifier before I laboriously filled each of the tanks and the innumerable plastic containers. Never an easy job, refuelling *Mabel E.Holland* in tropical heat was a task I dreaded.

After several excellent meals with friends, I decided to tear myself away on 11th October. Leaving was not made easier by the fact that a boy of about eight called Henry, whose father was Second Engineer on the ship I had been lying alongside, had made the lifeboat his playground for several days and was heartbroken that he could not come with me!

From Port Moresby it is about 200 miles to Bramble Cay, a small, isolated coral sand spit in the middle of the ocean which it is essential to find in order to pick up the channel at the Bligh Entrance of the Torres Strait. Accurate navigation is needed or one can easily end up on one of the reefs. At about 4pm on the 13th I picked up the tower on Bramble Cay and an hour and a half later came to anchor just a few yards from the sand spit in about 37m (120ft) of water. There were five fishing boats there and in a short while one of them sent over a small boat as the skipper recognized *Mabel* from when she had anchored in exactly the same spot in 1984!

In no time I was on board meeting Al, Speedy and Katie plus Tony and Robin from *Wild Fire* who were amazed to discover I had done another lap since last seeing them and we all sat down to supper and a good yarn together. Next morning, with a nice big Spanish mackerel in a bucket for my supper, I was on my way again down the North-East Channel leaving Dalrymple Island shimmering in the heat haze on my port side.

Then following a couple of days of island-hopping through the Torres Strait and Flinders Channel until I reached Thursday Island which is just off Cape York, the most northerly point of Australia. Here I could obtain clearance from Australian customs and immigration authorities who for some unknown reason confiscated my eggs, Parmesan cheese, tins of chicken paste, beans and pork. Australians can rest assured that they have not been contaminated by my Pommie tinned pork.

Thursday Island was the jumping-off point to cross the Gulf of Carpentaria on my way to Darwin. As I passed Cape Wessel and entered the Arafura Sea it became calm and unbearably hot, the thermometer showing 115°F inside the cabin. By the 22nd I reached Darwin and the following morning went alongside the Government Jetty to make my number with the harbour master who turned out to be an ex-pat named Jim Mayor who had once been coxswain of the Calshot Lifeboat. Feeling that we had something in common I asked his advice about laying up the lifeboat at Darwin. It was now only a week from the official beginning of the cyclone season and I did not feel the boat was really in a fit state to tackle a tropical storm in the Indian Ocean.

Jim Mayor suggested I see Bruce Perkins whose firm Perkins Shipping has a big depot where there might be an empty spot. Bruce proved most forthcoming and offered me a free space provided I could arrange a contractor to lift the boat out. This was easily organized the following day when Brambles' big mobile crane lifted the lifeboat and set her down on some concrete beams so there would be working space underneath, if needed. The Port Authority provided lengths of chain to secure the boat to the concrete beams as it is advisable to leave everything well tied down in the cyclone season – even a 20-ton lifeboat! My next call was to Roddy Montgomery, known as 'Mr Shade' because he makes a special shade cloth which lets air through but keeps off the burning tropical sun which would be extremely damaging to a wooden hull over a period of months.

My old friends Norman and Kay Turner, who were building a home for themselves in Darwin came and helped me to drape the shade cloth over a framework of plastic piping. Norm is one of those fastidious people who can do any job with his hands to perfection and he helped me greatly in servicing the engines and laying up all the machinery. I off-loaded about 500 gallons of fuel in cans into a spare shipping container which made life easier for maintenance work on board.

In the second week of November, having made all as safe as I knew how, I caught a flight for Heathrow and was glad to escape from the seething heat and humidity of Darwin. From the Australian summer I returned to the English winter and went back to the normal office routine until April 1990 when I flew out to prepare *Mabel* for the final part of her long journey home.

On returning to Darwin I was once again hit by the stifling humidity but found *Mabel E.Holland* none the worse for wear and with the shade cloth still intact. I had a relatively short list of jobs to do including antifouling the bottom, end-for-ending the propeller shafts and further improving the pumping arrangements.

Before doing those jobs I flew down to Sydney at the invitation of Don McIntyre who had been so incredibly helpful during my first two circumnavigations in *Ocean Bound*. He had asked me to officially launch his campaign for the forthcoming BOC single-handed round the world race. I could not have been more pleased to do so, though I am not sure how successful I was as a money-raiser as Don actually started the race with his boat named *Sponsor Wanted* and only changed it to *Buttercup* half way round. Anyway Don gave me a great time in Sydney and took me sailing on this exciting new 55-footer.

After this enjoyable 'time out' I returned to Darwin and completed making *Mabel E.Holland* ready for launching. On the 27th April Brambles Cranes put her back into the water and I commenced loading up with the help of Roddy Montgomery and a team of scouts. After one false start when a shaft ran hot and the SatNav broke down, I was on my way westwards on Thursday, 3rd May, 1990.

On my previous circumnavigation, the Timor Sea had been very calm and so it proved to be this time. The main hazard was the numerous fishing boats which, following Murphy's Law, always appeared at night. But after a couple of days they dropped astern and it becomes a more-or-less uninterrupted passage of a little over 1,000 miles to Christmas Island which I reached on the 13th. The purpose of calling there was to top up with fuel for the long hop to Mauritius but I also took the opportunity to visit the National Park and photograph the famous Coconut, Red and Blue land-crabs. I was befriended by an eccentric 72-year old named Alf Page who claimed to be a 'paper millionaire' on the basis of shares he owned in a gold-mine at Lasseter's Lost Reef. I had to turn down his request for a lift back to England, however.

From Christmas Island I launched off into the Indian Ocean, passing close by the Cocos (Keeling) Islands on the 20th May. It was winter now and the weather was pretty good initially with winds up to force 5 out of the north-east which would have been perfect if I had been sailing. About the third week in May the wind went round to the south-east and began to increase until it reached gale force during the last two days of an 18-day passage to Mauritius. It was a relief to stop the engines and experience quiet and stillness after such a long non-stop run.

The great pleasure of this part of the voyage was in meeting old acquaintances at the various ports. In Port Louis Harbour, Mauritius, Christian Wan and Edmond Quirin at the Taylor Smith shipyard welcomed me as long-lost friends. They wasted no time moving *Mabel E.Holland* alongside their dock and expertly smoothed my passage through customs and immigration formalities. Christian insisted on organizing work parties to carry out various jobs on board, including repainting the bulwarks which were looking distinctly tatty.

Mauritius is a fascinating island with some superb beaches and expensive tourist hotels which make a dramatic contrast with Port Louis with its open drains, hand-cart transport and dilapidated buildings. The place was busy trying to smarten itself up in anticipation of a visit from President Mitterand of France. I left on the 11th of June in much calmer conditions than when I arrived.

I was now heading for Durban, giving the south coast of Madagascar a wide berth of around 120 miles as the weather in this area can be volatile. The BBC World Service on short-wave stopped me from being totally out of touch with civilization and on the 16th I noted in the log a programme on the Queen's Birthday Honours, the Le Mans 24-hour race, World Cup football and Mike Tyson's big fight!

To reach Durban I had to cross the Agulhas Current which is said to produce some of the worst seas in the world. The current flows strongly to the south, parallel with the coastline, and kicks up a wicked sea if there is a strong wind from the opposite direction. I had a vivid illustration of this on the 22nd June when I was motoring steadily along in a moderate sea with a wind of about force 5 from the south-west. I had just been taking pictures of a school of pilot-whales when there was a sudden shower of heavy rain and within minutes the wind rose to 40 knots. In what seemed no time at all the boat was plunging into a heavy, breaking sea which seemed to appear from nowhere. With 40 miles to go to Durban I was thoroughly glad to be in boat built for bad weather as *Mabel E.Holland* breasted her way confidently over these distinctly impressive seas.

To my considerable relief I reached Durban safely at 5pm, and made fast at the crowded International Jetty. However this was not the end to the dramas of the day as after I had finished a meal at the yacht club and was enjoying the luxury of sleep in a bunk that did not constantly heave and sway, something caused me to wake. I thought I was dreaming of dripping water and with the watchfulness that becomes automatic after years of single-handed sailing, jumped up to find the source of this noise. To my astonishment I found myself looking at a black man crouching down by the steering wheel. Afterwards I realized the 'dripping water' was the sound of clinking money as he went through my trouser pockets. When I challenged him he spun me a story about being hungry and wanting to shelter from the cold so I gave him some food and sent him on his way.

When I related this incident at the yacht club, everyone was aghast and said I was extremely lucky not to have been knifed which is what usually happens when these people are disturbed. I had a number of friends in Durban including Alistair and Davina Campbell who run the ham radio network there and invited me for a relaxing weekend at their house. I also had happy reunions with my cousin Mike Dove and his family and Chris and Libby Bonnet at the Durban Sailing Academy.

The secret of rounding the bottom of South Africa is to wait for a depression to come through and set off as soon as the south-westerly wind eases and swings round to the north-east. The Agulhas current can then be used like a moving pavement as it gives a lift of up to five knots. I had a good, fast run down to East London and Port Elizabeth but after that it began to blow again and I took refuge in Plettenburg Bay for 24 hours. But on 5th July, my son Freddie's birthday, I rounded Cape Agulhas in fine, clear weather which continued until I reached Cape Town next day and berthed at the Royal Cape Yacht Club.

Here, I had the boat hauled out for cleaning and antifouling in preparation for the final leg of the journey. I was in no rush to leave Cape Town which has always been one of the most hospitable places I have visited and there were lots of friends to be looked up. When the boat was ready, the local TV station asked me to take them out to shoot some footage but unfortunately two of them were seasick as it was quite rough outside the harbour. After so many months at sea I had grown accustomed to *Mabel E.Holland*'s corkscrew motion which is certainly not one to encourage a weak stomach.

After a fortnight I was off again with St Helena the next destination, after a brief stop at Saldanha Bay to wait for the weather to improve. This passage was fairly uneventful and each day I passed some of the time in radio schedules with various 'ham' friends such as Owen who I had recently met at Saldanha Bay, Ros in Durban and Peter (PY1 ZAK) in Brazil. The amateur radio band is a reassuring lifeline as well as being a world-wide gossip-exchange.

St Helena is a delight to visit as it is full of historical interest. While there I walked to Plantation House, the Governor's residence and Longwood, one of the places where Napoleon was exiled. I did not take on any fuel at St Helena as I had already arranged to do so at Ascension Island which I reached on 11th August after an easy four-day passage. I planned to take on a full load at Ascension, sufficient to last me the whole way home to England and this was to be obtained from the fuelling ship which is permanently stationed at the island.

On arrival I made contact with the *Maersk Ascension* whose captain, John Lowe asked me to bring *Mabel E.Holland* to the stern of his ship where she could lie off on a long warp. A small boat took me to the ship's pilot ladder and I was welcomed by Captain Lowe and his officers at an excellent lunch. Next morning they passed down a hose and began filling my tanks at a nice slow rate. That part was easy but filling all the plastic containers was made harder by the fact that there was a considerable swell in the anchorage and *Mabel* rolled heavily on the end of her warp. Next day Captain Lowe had arranged to take me ashore for visits to the Administrator John Beal and the RAF station. Meanwhile his First Mate John volunteered to start work on filling the 240 fuel cans.

When we returned to the ship at about 3pm, after a rather good lunch at the RAF officer's mess, I was somewhat embarrassed to find the fuelling crew still at work. It turned out that the Taiwanese seamen quickly became sea-sick aboard *Mabel* and John the Mate had had to swap crews five times during the day. I therefore took over this task and after a further two hours completed loading the boat to her absolute maximum of nearly 1,100 gallons of diesel. After that I went on board the ship for a clean-up and about 20 people from the base came aboard for a party. After a further day of preparation and with many thanks to the crew of *Maersk Ascension* I was ready to cast off and set course for Madeira.

The lengthy passage through the tropics and up to Madeira took 17 days. The less said about Madeira the better. The harbour was filthy and the marina full with no visitor's berth kept free as is the custom in most parts of the world. If I had needed fuel it would have proved impossible and there was a fiasco with Customs over a replacement VHF radio which had been sent out to me. The cost of clearance was going to be more than the cost of the set and I ended up leaving it behind.

I was therefore not sorry to set off again on 4th September, bound for the River Tyne. Strong north-east winds blew for most of the passage, just in case I should be finding life too easy. One consolation was that radio conditions were excellent and I was able to make regular contact with Ros in Durban, Peter in Rio de Janeiro and Matt in New Zealand. *Mabel E.Holland* gradually rose in the water as the heavy load of fuel was used up and was just about on her marks by the time I reached Dartmouth, having motored 3,750 miles from Ascension Island.

Dartmouth was a quick 'unofficial' stop to clear Customs and take on some fuel before continuing up Channel and into the North Sea where I sneaked into the Alde for a private family reunion away from the crowds. In telephone calls from

Dartmouth, I had undertaken to arrive in Newcastle on Monday 24th September and to make sure nothing could go wrong I actually spent the Sunday night at anchor just outside the Tynemouth breakwater. Then at 9 next morning when I had tidied up the boat and put on a clean shirt, the Tyne Pilot launch and a flotilla of yachts arrived to escort me up river to St Peters Basin, Newcastle.

Mabel E.Holland had been away for four-and-a-half years and covered approximately 29,000 nautical miles. During that time she had forced her way through the most difficult and dangerous places that a boat can reach on this globe; had sunk, been raised, experienced temperatures from $+49°$ to $-60°C$ ($+120°$ to $-140°F$), suffered every kind of hard use imaginable and at the end of it all had brought me safely home, her venerable Gardner engines still in perfect order – a vessel with a stout heart. It was an emotional moment indeed as I steered her carefully through the lock-gate of the new Barratts Marina in the heart of Newcastle to receive a terrific welcome from family and friends, the Lord Mayor, a children's choir and band. We were home!

Postscript

After returning from Darwin, I learnt from Rick Thomas' girlfriend Rebecca Neame the following tragic story. After completing their transit of the Northwest Passage, Rick and his Kiwi friends went to British Columbia to pursue their other love; mountaineering. On the 13th September 1989, while at 10,000ft on Mount Waddington, Rick was caught in a rock-fall. A rock struck him on the head and he never regained consciousness. He had enjoyed his triumph in being first Briton through the Northwest Passage for a little over one month.

The following year the world of arctic navigation suffered another heart-felt loss when Capt. Tom Pullen died. More than anyone else, he had assisted me in undertaking the Northwest Passage and constantly gave me advice and the benefit of his very great experience of the area. Only a few weeks before his death he had been enthusiastically corres-ponding with myself and David Pelly about this book and forwarded a mass of useful information which has been of great help.

And what of the indefatigable *Mabel E. Holland*? Some time after our return to Newcastle, she received a royal visit when the Princess of Wales came to formally open the Bar-ratts Marina. Even before this I had been looking for a 'good home' for *Mabel*'s retirement as I was not keen to sell the boat which had served me so faithfully.

A major refit would be needed if she were to undertake another long voyage and I felt that perhaps the time had come when she could be allowed an honourable retirement.

And if *Mabel* has earned an honourable retirement, what of her master? My appetite for the far oceans has still not been quenched and at the time of writing I was hoping to acquire another boat to go in search of further adventures.

Index